Breeding & Raising Angelfishes

Edward Stansbury

Breeding & Raising Angelfishes

Project Team
Editor: Brian Scott
Copy Editor: Carl Schutt
Design: Candida Tomassini

T.F.H. Publications
President/CEO: Glen S. Axelrod
Executive Vice President: Mark E. Johnson
Publisher: Christopher T. Reggio
Production Manager: Kathy Bontz

T.F.H. Publications, Inc.
One TFH Plaza
Third and Union Avenues
Neptune City, NJ 07753

Cover image by Mr. Takashi Amano

Library of Congress Cataloging-in-Publication Data
Stansbury, Ed.
Breeding & raising angelfishes / Ed Stansbury.
p. cm.
Includes index.
ISBN 0-7938-0563-5 (alk. paper)
1.   Scalare. I. Title: Breeding and raising angelfishes. II. Title.
SF458.A5S73 2004
639.3'774--dc22
2004011276

This book has been published with the intent to provide accurate and authoritative information in regard to the subject matter within. While every precaution has been taken in preparation of this book, the author and publisher expressly disclaim responsibility for any errors, omissions, or adverse effects arising from the use or application of the information contained herein. The techniques and suggestions are used at the reader's discretion and are not to be considered a substitute for veterinary care. If you suspect a medical problem consult your veterinarian.

The Leader In Responsible Animal Care For Over 50 Years!™
www.tfhpublications.com

Contents

Purpose of This Book

There has been a need for a book like this for a long time, one that explains the process of obtaining pairs of angelfishes, successful spawning, and the raising and selling of the young. It is no secret that freshwater angelfishes are by far the best known of all the cichlids—except for perhaps the Oscar—and yet there have been few good books on their care and breeding for many years.

Unlike its predecessors, this book is full of reliable information and solid techniques that have been proven time and time again by more than one hobbyist with regard to the care of angelfish in aquariums. The author has gone into great depth on the breeding, genetics, and growing out of juvenile angelfishes. Further, he has taken great pains to identify and correct some of the myths that have arisen over the years surrounding their successful long-term care and breeding. Before we get to how to breed them and raise their young, it is important to understand what an angelfish is and where they come from.

Introduction

The family Cichlidae is comprised of many species, including the few relevant to this book—the freshwater angelfishes. Freshwater angelfishes are restricted to one contemporary genus—*Pterophyllum*. Within *Pterophyllum*, there are three valid species: *P. altum*, *P. leopoldi*, and *P. scalare*. Of these, only one is the real subject of this text, and that is *P. scalare*.

Pterophyllum altum

The deep angelfish, *Pterophyllum altum* (Pellegrin, 1903), is a highly sought after species that has the reputation for being one of the hardest cichlids to spawn successfully in aquariums. Certainly there are isolated reports of such events occurring; however, they frequently end with the failure to raise most or any of the fry to maturity.

Deep angels are a larger-growing species attaining lengths of 5 inches to 6 inches total length (TL) as adults and nearly 12 inches in height. Their feeding habits are almost identical to other angelfishes, with the only exception being their need for more food because they grow a little larger. There are two main populations from where most of the specimens imported into the United States originate. The first and most sought after population occurs within the Orinoco River basin in Venezuela. The second population, which may become a distinct species in the future, is native to the upper Rio Negro and its associated tributaries in northern Brazil.

Pterophyllum leopoldi

Leopold's angel, *Pterophyllum leopoldi* (Gosse, 1963), is a relatively unknown species to many hobbyists. They are sought after by collectors specializing in rare cichlids or by hobbyists wishing to set up geographically-correct aquariums from one of the fish's limited geographical areas.

Some of the most striking displays housing Leopold's angels are those that recreate the Rio Manacapuru in Brazil. Oftentimes, these displays have large specimens of the Manacapuru blue discus, *Symphysodon aequifasciata*, and they may also include clouds of schooling cardinal tetras, *Paracheirodon axelrodi*, along with an assortment of *Corydoras* species as clean-up crews. The diet, husbandry, and size of Leopold's angels are nearly identical to those of the silver angel and should be kept according to the guidelines contained herein.

Pterophyllum scalare

The common freshwater angelfish, *Pterophyllum scalare* (Lichtenstein, 1823), is commonly called the "silver angel" by hobbyists in the United States. They are a medium-sized cichlid indigenous to the waters of northern Brazil, Colombia, and Peru where they sometimes cohabitate with the other members of their genus or at least back right up to them in their distribution in various waterways, lagoons, and lakes.

Silver angels reach a maximum size in nature of approximately 4 inches in TL and around 6 inches to 8 inches in height. They may grow slightly larger in aquariums due to regular feedings and little competition for food in most cases. They can be long-lived, with specimens commonly reaching six or more years of age. They prefer temperatures in the upper 70s to mid-80s degrees Fahrenheit but can live and even breed in temperatures several degrees Fahrenheit in either direction and even as low as 67°F.

In nature, freshwater angelfish commonly inhabit swamps and flooded forests (seasonal) where there is an abundance of aquatic vegetation and the water is either very clear or just slightly silty. They feed heavily on invertebrates such as insect larvae, water fleas (*Daphnia*), and other types of freshwater crustaceans. In aquariums, they will take a vast assortment of foodstuffs, as you will soon read about in the chapter dealing with diet and nutrition.

Pterophyllum scalare, the silver angelfish.

1

Environmental Requirements

The most important environmental requirements that hobbyists should be familiar with includes aquariums, water quality, oxygen content, temperature, lighting (photoperiod), and nutrition. All of these are very familiar to the advanced hobbyist, but perhaps not completely understood by the novice fishkeeper breeding angelfish for the first time. For these reasons it is important to carefully explain each of these topics below except for nutrition, which requires a whole chapter to itself due to its complexity and high importance.

Aquariums

While there is nothing unusual about the aquariums themselves, there are some suggestions about which sizes to use. Small angelfishes require quite a lot of space while growing into adulthood in order to achieve their full size and strength. This size is necessary for good breeding stock, and the strength is necessary for the stress of mating and breeding. Thus, youngsters being grown for future breeders should be given as much space as you can afford and I suggest at least a 50-gallon aquarium for 12 to 15 fish. As they approach breeding size and age, they should be trimmed down to half this many in the same 50-gallon aquarium. For pairs, few (if any) breeders would suggest any aquarium smaller than a 15-gallon and many would recommend at least one capable of holding 20 gallons.

The eggs can be hatched in a container of almost any size. I remember my father hatching angelfish eggs in shallow plastic dishes, bread pans, etc., almost 50 years ago. Some people recommend clear glass 1-gallon jugs, others recommend 5-gallon to 15-gallon aquariums. They are all suitable, but for the sake of saving space, the 1-gallon jugs are probably best. My most dependable sources for these jugs are restaurants, school cafeterias, etc.

Once the eggs have hatched and the young are free swimming, they must be housed in much larger quarters. Aquariums holding 10 or 15 gallons will suffice for now but will need to be increased as the young grow. For raising young to saleable size, various people recommend different sized aquariums. One

Beware of Chlorine

If your water is chlorinated, you may want to use a dechlorinating agent, which may be purchased from your local aquarium shops. The active ingredient in these products is usually sodium thiosulphate. However, this product is certainly not a necessity for every hobbyist or breeder. Simply aerating the water or just letting it stand in open containers will allow the chlorine to leave the water and pass into the air in less than 24 hours or so. In addition, you can add small amounts of chlorinated water to your tanks without harm to the fish. I try to refrain from adding more than about 15% chlorinated water at any one time. Because your chlorine level is probably fluctuating from time to time, you may want to ask local hobbyists about their experiences with chlorine or do some experimenting on your own.

Even though bare aquariums are more practical, it's hard to beat the look of healthy angels in a nicely planted aquarium.

breeder uses 10-gallon aquariums, raising about 75 youngsters in each. I prefer moving the young into 50-gallon aquariums after the initial raising period. Within these recommended sizes, choose the size with which you are familiar, or the sizes that best fit your fish room and rack design, or, if you are short of cash or other resources, choose the ones you presently have and make do until you can do better. In each case, set up the bare aquariums with airstones, corner filters, or sponge filters.

The advantages of a bare aquarium are numerous. First, the bare aquarium allows you to monitor exactly how much food your fish are eating and how much is being wasted. Second, they show all the feces and other particulates so you can remove them. Third, bare aquariums are also much less trouble to run and less expensive to set up. Once you get used to seeing the actual condition of the tank, you may never want to use a furnished tank again.

A Closer look At Water Changes

In order to determine the effects of water changes on breeder angels, I conducted the following informal experiment. I ran 60 pairs of breeder angels in 15-gallon tanks and used three different water change schedules. When water changes were done, tank bottoms were siphoned and the water was replaced slowly from an overhead gravity system. The first 20 pairs received a 20% water change every day. These fish were very disturbed by the intrusion and acted nervous and unsettled, but the spawning rate remained high. The second 20 pairs received water changes of 20% every third day. These pairs had time to settle down after each siphoning, seemed very content, and had the highest spawning rate of any group. The third group of 20 breeders had inside box filters and water changes of 50% once a week. This group had the worst spawning rate, worst water conditions, and the poorest appetites.

Because of this, I tried to continue water changes once every third day and included box filters with airstones to guarantee good water quality. I encourage you to do your own experiments. Because the room you have for your fish and your routines are certainly quite different from mine, you may get different results.

With water changes, pH and hardness should take care of themselves. As long as your water is soft (between 80 and 150 ppm or so—this is very approximate!) and your pH is between 6.8 and 7.6, you should be well within the range of water conditions that will provide breeding success. These ranges are not sacred, but they do provide a range that has proven successful for numerous hobbyists and breeders, including myself.

Water Quality

Water quality is very important for the hobbyist to understand. The quality of the water in which you are housing your angelfishes must remain within certain limits in order to raise their young and keep broodstock healthy. All of the basics of good aquarium keeping apply. You must use mechanical, biological, and chemical filtration, or you must change enough water on a regular basis to perform the same function that a filter providing multi-step filtration would do.

Mechanical Filtration

Mechanical filtration can be provided to angels of all ages through the use of box or sponge filters. Each of these filters also provides some biological purification by providing some surface area for bacterial action on nitrogenous wastes. While it is common to hear many hobbyists tout the biological filtration abilities of sponge filters, I remain unconvinced of their usefulness for breeding tanks. They are poor biological filters because they need cleaning long before bacteria are able to establish efficient nitrification. I would like to suggest that the real value of these small filters in any aquarium is oxygenation

Small angels should have a good mechanical filter running at all times on their aquarium. Blushing angels are pictured here.

The best way to ensure a high level of dissolved oxygen is through the use of airstones.

and particle filtration. Because all vertebrate animals require oxygen, it's not too surprising that oxygen plays a very important role in fish health. The need for an understanding of the role of oxygen is even more vital because we are talking about growing fish in as crowded conditions as possible in order to maximize hatchery efficiency.

High oxygen levels provide some protection for the damage that could be caused by high ammonia levels. Apparently, the oxygen and ammonia/nitrite molecules compete for binding sites on the hemoglobin molecules in the blood within the vessels of the gills. The more oxygen there is, the better it competes with these pollutants. Many studies show this protective effect of oxygen at the saturation level in water and the predisposition to disease that occurs whenever oxygen levels fall below this level. This evidence should not be ignored.

The best way of ensuring high oxygen levels is to use airstones or the inexpensive box filters that use airstones. If you are using a large air compressor or air blower, be sure it has an air filter on it. This will help ensure clean air is getting to the stones. Without this air filtration, the airstones will quickly become clogged with dust and will be useless because you will think that you have good oxygen levels, when in reality you do not.

Even with these precautions, the airstones will slowly clog from their own grit filling the pores. The stones are cheap and plentiful; simply plan on replacing them every few months or so. Meanwhile, have an oxygen test kit handy and use it periodically to monitor the tanks and to test the water when things go wrong (diseases, unexplained deaths, etc.).

Test the oxygen level from your water source, whether it is well or city water, and you will probably find that the level is quite a bit below saturation. Saturation varies with temperature, but should be about 5.5 mg of oxygen per liter of water at an aquarium temperature of about 80°F. Test your various tanks regularly and record the data. You will now have "norms" for your water and hatchery tanks to use for future reference.

It is not worth your effort to identify all of the polluting chemicals produced in your tank through biological and chemical processes. The capability to cheaply filter out all of these pollutants does not exist. Consequently, the time-proven

You will need excellent water quality to grow your angels out to adulthood—like this adult gold marble.

Altum angels are notorious for their sensitivity to poor water quality and failure to adapt to a captive lifestyle. If you choose to keep altum angels, proceed with caution.

method of ensuring the highest water quality is water changes. This dilutes all pollutants, irritants, and built-up salts, stabilizes long-term water quality, stimulates appetite, reproductive activity, and seems to act as a general tonic for the fish. As long as the temperature and pH changes are small, the results are therapeutic. Again, this follows the modern concept of good aquarium management.

Temperature

Many aquarists are under the impression that tropical fishes must be kept at 80°F. This is certainly not so. Angelfishes can be bred and can certainly be maintained in water as low as 74°F. I have even seen angels breed at 67°F, although I certainly do not recommend it. The most important thing is that the temperature must remain stable. There are, however, some species of angelfish, such as the altum angel

(*Pterophyllum altum*), that require very high temperatures to breed successfully in aquariums. Thus, be sure of what species of angelfish you have so you can adjust your captive environment accordingly.

One interesting sidelight on temperature is the recent scientific evidence that abrupt temperature changes are detrimental. Changes as little as one degree will cause hormonal changes that indicate shock and will last for days. You may get away with changing the tank water's temperature more than this, but you are pushing your luck and often shocking your fish unnecessarily.

Test Kits

For monitoring various water quality parameters, buy and use test kits. They are available for testing everything from dissolved oxygen, ammonia, nitrite, nitrate, pH, both calcium and carbonate hardness, and even less critical environmental factors, such as carbon dioxide. I would also recommend buying a copper test kit if you use copper for the treatment of disease (i.e. velvet or ick). Environmental quality is closely linked to fish health. Therefore, any tools that help you understand your water quality will enable you to produce better fish with fewer disease problems. Compared to the cost of the fish you will be able to save, the cost of these kits is very cheap indeed.

2

Diet & Nutrition

The nutritional requirements of fishes are still largely unknown, with research being done mostly on the commercially valuable fish such as tilapia, trout, salmon, and channel catfish. However, some generalizations can be made from this research to help the hobbyist in the selection of proper foods and the elimination of inappropriate foods. First, it is necessary to review the little that is known about tropical fish nutrition.

General Nutrition of Fishes

All food constituents necessary for health are divided into groups based on structure or function. These categories include proteins, fats, carbohydrates, minerals, vitamins, and water. Water is rarely a problem nutritionally for fishes because of its absorption from the aquatic environment and consumed foods. Precise vitamin and mineral requirements are unknown for almost all fishes and would be very difficult for the hobbyist to measure, monitor, or control. In addition, fishes assimilate minerals largely through their gill membranes and not through their foods. For these reasons, many outdoor hatcheries rely on the naturally occurring pond life and mineral content of the water in order to supply minimum amounts of vitamins and minerals.

The three remaining nutrient classes are well defined over a broad range of species and can be discussed in a little more detail. When foods are consumed, the associated proteins are then broken down by digestive enzymes into amino acids. These components are used for energy or for reassembly into new proteins. These proteins are then used in building nearly all of the body tissues. Through many scientifically conducted feeding trials, protein levels ranging from 26% to 60% of the dry weight of feed have proven to be adequate for growth in many fish species. These specific tests have not involved angels but have been done on other cichlids (i.e., tilapia). High levels of protein are of no advantage and can be deadly.

Fats include both solid fats and liquid oils. These compounds supply at least twice the energy of carbohydrates or proteins per unit of weight and are stored in fish tissues for reserve energy. It is well established that fishes do not effectively utilize hard, high melting-point fats. However, fishes readily digest low melting-point fats, compounds you think of as oils.

Rapidly growing fishes utilize oils in preference to carbohydrates as their primary source of energy. Experimentally acceptable oil levels range from 4% to 40% dry weight, with 15% to 25% being optimum for growth in trout. Oxygen present reacts with oils, turning them rancid, toxic, and therefore unusable for feeding. The last nutrient is carbohydrates. Carbohydrates may be in the form of starches or sugars. Starches are not easily digested and are not utilized for energy in most fishes. They can, however, be very dangerous; levels of 33% carbohydrates can cause liver damage in trout. Low levels of sugars (less than 10%) are a readily digestible and valuable source of energy in fishes that have been studied.

Nutrition is very important to rearing your baby angels successfully. Be sure to provide only the best foods to them.

Natural Dietary Requirements

In nature, most fishes feed on a large variety of organisms, including algae, crustaceans, adult and larval insects, other fishes, snails, and plants. Any imbalance of nutrients from one food tends to be counterbalanced by the nutrients in other foods. Every species is adapted to its natural diet. This adaptation can be understood in terms of where a fish feeds. Is it a surface feeder, a middle-level feeder, a bottom feeder, or a mixture. (i.e., pursuit predator)? Each of these habitats provides a different assortment of foods and provides the hobbyist with clues to dietary needs.

Note the deep red color of this altum angel's eye— a sign of good health and vigor.

Morphological and physiological clues regarding the shape of the body are important as well: Is it built for short, quick bursts of speed needed by predators, or is it flattened on the underside and therefore adapted to life on the bottom? Other physiological clues might include whether the stomach space is present, as is required by fish eating large amounts of protein, or whether the digestive tract is long and undifferentiated for slow digestion of plants and algae (i.e., *Tropheus* sp.).

Replacing fishes' natural diets with an artificial diet is often undesirable yet unavoidable when it comes to most fishes housed in aquariums. It therefore pays to understand your fishes' natural diet and how to match it with similar kinds of available foods.

Just what do we know about the natural feeding habits of our particular fish? Take angelfishes, for example. Unfortunately, we don't know very much. There are a few reports and observations dealing with various aspects of wild populations of angels that describe them actively feeding on algae along the riverbanks. Omnivores, like swordtails and platys, have gut lengths about one and a half times their body length. True herbivores have gut lengths many times their body lengths, and true predators may have gut lengths less than a body length.

Angels have a gut length about equal to their body length, which suggests they are predators with omnivorous tendencies. Also, angels have strong teeth and a true stomach capable of handling some amounts of protein. These are clues. Do we have direct evidence? Yes, in a way. What we really have is empirical evidence from hundreds of hobbyists worldwide who have written articles over the last 40 years. Their breeding experiences show that angels have a real liking for all normal conditioning foods, such as live adult brine shrimp, *Tubifex* worms, white worms, *Daphnia*, *Cyclops*, chopped earthworms, mealworms, fruit flies, mosquito larvae, and others. Watching them hunt down other fishes, like baby guppies, indicates they are skillful and instinctive pursuit predators, too.

Types of Foods for Captive Angelfishes

Most aquarists, however, have no trouble maintaining healthy angels without the use of any live foods at all. How, then, do you choose which foods to feed to your angels? In order to choose among the forms of foods (flake, frozen, freeze dried, and live), you need to examine some of the pros and cons of each.

Prepared Foods

Dry flake foods are popular because they are easy to use and store. They are adequate for many fishes with low nutritional

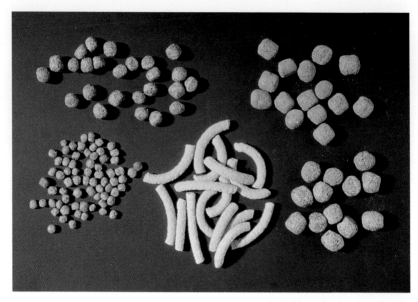

Pelleted foods provide a good staple diet for angels, just make sure they are not too big to fit in their mouths.

needs. Think of them as maintenance foods. Dry foods provide proteins, carbohydrates, vitamins, and minerals if they are processed correctly. The process of making flakes is quite simple. First, a wet mixture (like a milkshake) is made of the food constituents, which are then sprayed onto hot revolving drums. The thin material is quickly cooked and dried and falls off the drum as uniformly thin flakes. Because of the high heat involved, many vitamins are broken down and are worthless to the fishes. Extra vitamins must be added to the flakes after drying in order for them to be a valuable food source. For those companies that will not tell you how they make their flakes, you should assume the worst. Not all flake foods are made to high manufacturing standards. Choose with care!

Also, because these foods are often stored for long periods of time, their fat content is very low in order to avoid having the product become rancid through contact with atmospheric oxygen. Consequently, flake foods cannot provide adequate fats for adults or fast-growing youngsters. Another drawback may be very high proportions of carbohydrates, so be sure to check the labels.

Freeze-dried Foods

Freeze-dried foods are also very popular because they are convenient to use and store. Freeze-drying is a very efficient method for preserving all of the nutrients present in the organism being processed except fats. Like dry foods, contact with oxygen during and after processing turns oils rancid. Also, some nutritional deficiencies may exist in the original organism and so would be absent in the freeze-dried product as well. The high cost of feeding this type of food is also prohibitive for its use in hatcheries.

Some freeze-dried foods can actually be pressed against the wall of the aquarium so the fish can pick at them.

Frozen Foods

Freezing is very efficient and effective for preserving all of the nutrients present in the organism. The nutritional benefits of frozen foods will only be limited by the natural content of the organism. Freezing is also the best method for preserving the oils in live foods. As more and more products become available for hobby use, especially in marine aquaria, more and better frozen foods are becoming commonplace, with the only drawback being expense.

Live Foods

Live foods have been the standard for conditioning and breeding excellence for decades. Live foods contain all of the nutrient classes, including oils. Because fishes are instinctively attracted to live foods' natural motions and odor, they tend to eat more, and therefore receive better nutrition. Culturing a variety of live foods is a bit difficult because of the time and expertise required. If purchased, live foods are far too expensive for most hobbyists that may require them in bulk, and the supplies are often not dependable because seasonality and other factors often influence their availability.

Years ago, hobbyists gathered live foods from every mucky pond they could find in an effort to condition and breed their exotic fishes. While they did get good results, they also picked up every strange, undiagnosable plague and parasite as well, often with counterproductive results. Today, there are even more problems with collecting live foods then there used to be, for example the presence of pesticides and herbicides. These are being sprayed over the entire world, interacting and accumulating in every biotope known. You can't see them, you can't test for them, but they will kill your fishes just the same.

Do not collect live foods regardless of how free or easy it seems to be. As you can see, there is no simple answer to the question, "What should I feed my fish?" For maintaining health, many of the convenience foods are adequate. For the hobbyist who wishes to breed angels, more deliberate thought is required. Broodstock requires large amounts of highly nutritious foods in order to produce large numbers of young over an extended period of time, and those young must receive the best foods if they are to grow rapidly and strongly.

The solution is to consciously choose a variety of foods utilizing all of the various forms as necessary to provide

Blackworms are very popular with angelfish breeders. Of course, as with any live food, be sure they are clean and healthy before offering them to your fish.

a complete and balanced diet. Tailor the diet to the fish, become aware of nutritional deficiencies in various foods and the various food forms, compensate by feeding a wide variety, and realize that the more you demand of your fish, the better nutrition the fish requires.

You may think that learning about fish nutrition to this extent is overkill. I am including this much material because I believe that more strides will be made in the next decades in improving fish diets and in understanding the importance of good nutrition than in any other part of the industry. If this is true, then you will be ahead of the game if you start learning the basics now.

Review of Foods

There are five nutrient categories to fulfill and four common food types.

- *Choose flake foods as a vitamin and mineral insurance policy and to provide some dietary bulk.*

- *Choose frozen foods to help provide vitamins, proteins, and fats. Different brands of frozen brine shrimp are available but in greatly different qualities. Choose the brand that holds together and doesn't have a lot of extraneous material in it.*

- *Choose freeze-dried foods to help with proteins, carbohydrates, vitamins, and minerals. It must be a food the fish will eat. Experiment to find out which products your angels will accept.*

- *Choose several live foods alternated throughout the week. Good choices include whiteworms,* Tubifex *or* Limnodrilus, *fruit flies, adult brine shrimp,* Daphina, *and bloodworms. The more live foods offered, the better, in my opinion.*

Feed a variety of foods from the above types, and you will assure adequate nutrition for adults and growing fry. The small, free-swimming babies should be fed newly hatched brine shrimp; anything else they eat is a bonus.

Also, you must keep costs in mind. You can make your own or grow your own. When you can buy in bulk to save money, then do it. The small sizes of commercial foods found at your local retailers are often inappropriate for large-scale enterprises. If you want to try bulk packages of foods, call the manufacturer or distributor and request quantities intended for hatchery use. Refrigeration or freezing is a must for preserving nutrients in these larger sizes of commercial foods.

Live Food Culture

In order to make the information readily available, I am including a few pages on culturing some live foods. These culturing methods are nearly foolproof, and I urge you to try them.

Whiteworms

Whiteworms (*Enchytraeus albidus*) are dwarf worms that have been collected worldwide and cultured for the conditioning of tropical fishes. These worms have both sets of sex organs in each individual (hermaphroditic), as do their larger cousins, the common earthworm. Cocoons are produced about once a week, with each cocoon carrying from 2 to 45 eggs depending on the age and condition of the adults. The young leave the cocoon after about 12 days and grow to maturity in about 21 days.

Nutritionally, whiteworms are superior to Tubifex or Daphnia as a source of proteins and fats essential for rapid growth and egg production. At the same time, they are low in unnecessary carbohydrates. They are a bit deficient in vitamins and minerals as compared to other foods, however.

Culturing whiteworms is very easy. Locate a proper storage place for your culture that provides a year-round temperature between 59° and 69°F. Outside of this temperature range they will not produce a vigorous culture. The worms reproduce best at 65°F. They can survive freezing but will not reproduce.

A very good culture box can be built out of unfinished ½-inch lumber or plywood. Nailing provides adequate strength. Box size is important because the box must hold enough soil so that the temperature and humidity remain constant. I have had the most success with boxes 8 inches to 12 inches square and 4 inches to 6 inches deep. Smaller boxes are better only if you have a very small population of worms.

These worms are hermaphroditic but not self-fertile. Therefore, reproduction is proportional to population density. Too few worms in too large a container will get lost and the worms cannot reproduce. It is important to cover the culture box, as it is vital for controlling moisture and soil humidity. Because these worms avoid light, a tight cover helps keep the culture dark and the worms at the surface of the soil. A good tight cover also protects the culture from invasion by various pests such as beetles, mice, and ants. The soil for the culture should be high in organic material and low in clays and sands.

Soil Mixtures

Commercial potting soils are excellent. The organic matter helps provide an acid soil condition favorable to the worms, as well as a texture that remains loose and retains moisture. Adding up to 50% vermiculite also contributes to a loose soil with capacity for holding moisture. Be careful that the commercial potting soil you choose does not contain chemicals for killing insects or insect eggs, fungi, or other similar pests. These additives will also kill the worms. Read the labels!

If you choose to make your own soil mixture, use sifted garden soil, peat moss, and vermiculite in equal proportions. The exact proportions are not critical. Before using, spread the mixture thinly on aluminum sheets and bake in an oven at 150°F for two to three hours to kill all pests and their eggs. Allow the soil to cool completely before use. Fill your culture boxes about 4 inches to 6 inches deep. Earthworms have a thick outer cuticle that prevents loss of water through the integument. Because whiteworms do not have this protective cuticle, they cannot regulate water gain or loss through their integument. This means that the air in and above the soil must remain at a constant 100% humidity to keep the worms from drying out.

Whiteworm Culture Tips

1. *Don't disturb the culture too often. This disruption inhibits growth and reproduction. It is best to harvest, feed, and water in a single operation, thereby reducing the number of times you disturb the culture.*

2. *If worms are gathered into a few large clumps at the soil surface, then the culture is probably too dry. Slowly, over the course of a week or two, increase the amount of water sprayed at each feeding until the worms spread uniformly across the surface.*

3. *If the worms are crawling up the sides to get out of the soil, then the soil is either too wet or the population of the box is too great or the culture needs to be split. If it is too wet, skip spraying when you feed. The dry breadcrumbs will help to soak up the excess moisture. Stir the soil in order to expose the wet soil on the bottom to the air at the surface. You should see improvement in just a few days.*

4. *If the worms do not gather at the top, then the culture is probably too dry or is not fed enough. Without food at the surface, the worms will move downward to find something to eat. Another possibility is that there is too much light, which can happen if you are using plastic or glass boxes. In order to block out some of the light, increase moisture at the surface, and help keep the worms at the top, add a piece of colored glass, slate, or plastic on the top of the soil. This will act as a moisture collector, a condensing surface for the moisture that will help keep the worms at the top.*

5. *If the culture is old or musty smelling or a sour smell is detected, the culture is polluted with bacteria and fungi. Divide the culture and add new soil mix.*

6. *If the soil seems to pack, there is too much clay. Divide the culture and add new soil mix with extra peat moss or vermiculite.*

7. *If the culture is infested with mites, you are probably overfeeding or not keeping the culture clean of uneaten scraps. A small population of mites is not necessarily harmful, but they do compete for food and contribute to polluting the soil.*

At the same time, the soil must never be soggy, as this would inhibit gas exchange throughout. Learning the proper moisture balance is the most difficult phase of culturing whiteworms. Beginners tend to keep cultures too dry. Water the culture after each harvesting or feeding by spraying lightly with a fine plant sprayer. Never pour water on the culture.

Feeding is no problem because research done on whiteworms indicates that white bread is one of the very best foods available. I prefer to dry the slices of white bread and then grind them into breadcrumbs. I sprinkle about one heaping tablespoon on the surface of the soil of an average culture every second or third day and mist lightly. Ideally, the amount of food consumed should increase over time. Never feed until all of the previous feeding is cleaned up! Uneaten food quickly becomes infested with bacteria and fungi that release inhibitors that will repel the worms. If the previous feeding is not entirely eaten, then either remove all particles of the old bread, or wait until the old food is eaten before feeding again.

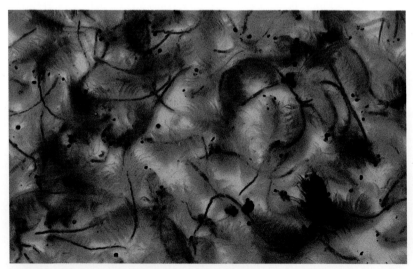

Brine shrimp are easy to obtain and fairly cheap. Those who wish to raise their own brine shrimp can do so by obtaining eggs from a local aquarium shop.

"Regardless of its nutritional benefits, a steady diet of any one food will be inadequate."

A worm population will reach a peak at about two months. If possible, wait until this time before feeding out of the culture. Also, the culture can be split in two at about this time. Simply divide the culture in half, adding one half of the culture to a new box. Then add new soil to each box. Mix the new soil into the boxes and begin feeding bread to the new culture. This will give you one box to feed fish from and one box that can be used to start new cultures. As long as the worms are fed at the soil surface, you should be able to gather clumps of mats of worms on or just under the surface. Clean the worms by placing them in a small dish of water. After 10 or 15 minutes, they should have purged themselves free of soil and partially digested food, and can be gathered in clean clumps in shallow water. They are now ready to be fed to breeders. A dozen worms per fish twice or three times a week is enough.

Brine Shrimp (*Artemia*)

Newly hatched brine shrimp have been the industry standard for feeding angel fry since the early 1950s. During the intervening years, high-quality eggs have almost always been easy to obtain, but there have been years where production was low.

More for Your Money

Brine shrimp eggs are not cheap; therefore, be sure that you have hatched out as many of the eggs as possible. To ensure this, the cone can be re-aerated and allowed (for a few more hours) to continue collecting extra shrimp that were slow to hatch and that escaped the first harvest.

Whenever possible, buy the eggs in number 10 cans. They are more economical when purchased this way. Store the opened cans in the freezer, where there is little or no humidity to damage the eggs. I have hatched eggs in small flat pans, every manner of jug and jar, and even inverted soda bottles. However, my brine shrimp needs and space constraints required more efficiency. This has led to my present system: using custom-made fiberglass cones, about 16 inches across the top and about 22 inches tall. Each of these could hold

> ## "Do not reuse the water from the cone or from the harvesting process. It is too high in pollutants and not worth saving."

about 7 or 8 gallons, but I fill each of them to about 5 gallons. This prevents slop-over. Into 5 gallons of tap water, I add 1 and $1/2$ cups of rock salt, $1/4$ cup of eggs, and strong aeration. I use enough air to guarantee that the eggs do not settle on the bottom of the cone. When the eggs hatch, the air is turned off the egg shells float,and the brine shrimp settle to the bottom, where they can be siphoned into a fine net, rinsed, and fed to the small fish.

Daphnia

Every hobbyist should take advantage of this wonderful live food. It can be easily cultured indoors year round or outdoors except in winter. Outdoors, I set up large tubs placed in direct sun, filled with water, and fertilized with plant fertilizer, a quart of partially decayed winter leaves, a quarter head of lettuce, or a cup of week-old cow manure. As soon as the water turns green with algae, you can introduce a small culture of Daphnia. You can usually find them for sale in stores, on the Internet, or trade for a culture from other hobbyists. The *Daphnia* eat the algae, and you can harvest nets full of live food from the tub until winter. Be sure to change the water regularly so as to keep the pollutants low.

Indoors, I have kept cultures going for years in spare 15-gallon tanks, with shop lights fitted with cool white tubes set on timers for 16 hour days. Simply make the algae in one tank, and feed all the other tanks with the algae. Do not use a brine shrimp net to collect your *Daphnia*. Use a porous net or sieve that will allow you to collect the adults, and allow the instars (young) to fall through. Again, change the water (*Daphnia* do not like acid water and will die with exposure to any trace of copper), and keep the algae coming.

The Feeding of Trout pellets

Against somewhat popular belief, trout pellets are not to be used with angels. I have seen people kill breeders and adults by feeding this "economical" food. In my experience, the angels eat this food and seem to do well. After a few months, they suddenly stop feeding and begin swelling up as if they had dropsy (dropsy usually acts fast, swelling the fish until the scales stick straight out from the body). The angels eating trout pellets never swell to this degree. They are listless, color very intensely, and may not die for a month or more after the symptoms start. In the last stages they become quite dark, lose their equilibrium, and die on the bottom. Pathologists consulted found various internal organs affected, such as fatty livers and hugely swollen spleens. Liver dysfunction is apparently the prime cause of death due to the balance of nutrients in trout chow compared with angelfish's dietary requirements. Aquarium fish food manufacturers have put a lot of research into the development of their foods, which are the best choice for aquarium fish; commercial aquaculture foods are designed for growing fish quickly to market size, not lifelong sustenance.

3

Genetics

The reproductive process is complex, but the end result is easy to understand. Each adult begins with two sets of chromosomes in each cell. However, in the reproductive cells, the chromosomes separate into two groups of chromosomes, with each set going to a different egg (or sperm).

Chance decides which eggs (or sperm) get the first set, and which eggs (or sperm) get the second set. The fertilized egg then combines 1/2 of the chromosomes from the female parent, and a different 1/2 from the male parent to yield the correct total.

Phenotypes

Phenotype refers to how an organism looks, while genotype refers to the genetic instructions an organism carries in its chromosomes. Identical twins are identical genotypes, yet the growth process, environment, and experience changes them ever so slightly so that they never look perfectly identical. These differences in appearance are phenotypic differences. When you look at two different kinds of angelfish, you are seeing phenotypic displays. For simplicity, I will use the terms type, kind, variety, line, and strain to mean major commercially important differences among angelfish.

The list of different kinds of angelfish phenotypes with which I have had some experience includes: silver, silver veil, marble, marble veil, gold, gold veil, blushing, blushing veil, black lace, black lace veil, black, black veil, smoky, smoky veil, ghost, ghost veil, zebra, zebra veil, leopard, leopard veil, clown, and clown veil.

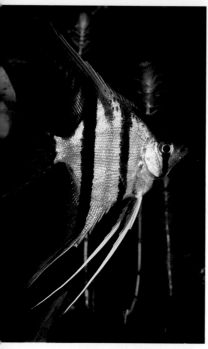

A wild-type angel, probably
Pterophyllum leopoldi.

Wild-Type Angels

The wild-type angel (silver angel) is the one that's found in nature. The body is grayish silver with three body stripes: one through the eye; one at the anterior part of the dorsal fin that extends across the body, ending between the pelvic fin and the start of the anal fin; and one stripe reaching from the tip of the dorsal fin down through the body to the tip of the anal fin. Often an extra, thin stripe is visible at the caudal peduncle, or short lines that come and go with mood, lighting, etc. may be seen among the other stripes. The body is not uniformly colored but has lighter shades along the ventral surface and darker shades of brown, black, or green along the dorsal half of the body.

Veil Angels

The first successful variety established was veils. Veils have extra long fin rays and membranes, giving the fish the extra grace and beauty we have come to expect in perfect angels. It also makes them slower, a bit more sluggish, and more prone to diseases such as fin and tail rot. The veil trait appeared in a line of silvers sometime in the mid-1950s. This is such an attractive trait that it is routine to "tack" these impressive fins onto all new angel mutations.

Half-Black Angels

Sometime in the late 1940s or early 1950s, the half-black appeared. This fish has normal silver coloring on the front half and black on the back half. These fish are difficult to raise, with light demand by the public, and are not often available.

Black Lace Angels

Black lace is a phenotype with a much darker body than that exhibited by silver angels. The fins are the same as those on silvers, while the stripes may be slightly

A young half-black angel.

darker or wider. The body looks as if it has a black to charcoal cast. These angels are called black lace because the blackening has a very beautiful effect on the rays and the membranes of the fins, giving them a lacy appearance. After the establishment of the black lace line, many hobbyists began trying to produce an all-black angel.

Black Angels

Black angels began appearing in the hobby in 1955. Black angels are basically a black lace crossed with a black lace, giving them more intense black coverage on their flanks. Their striped pattern is always apparent under the black. Since black angelfish were first produced, one of the goals of breeders has been to produce a uniformly black stripeless fish. One method of eliminating any evidence of striping is to raise the young in constant light. This gives the fish a solid black body with no stripes. Another method of producing a black fish without body stripes is to cross a gold blushing with a black gold blushing, giving about one half the spawn a black, stripeless appearance.

A juvenile blusher.

This is a classical marble angel.

Ghost Angels

In 1961, another sport called a ghost angel was found. This mutation did not have any black body stripes, but the small eye stripe was still present. In most of the articles about breeding, and throughout this book, the ghost gene is called a stripeless gene.

Blushing Angels

In 1965, a fish was introduced with very little pigmentation in the skin or fins. The skin of this fish is transparent, including the gill covers, which allows the red gills to show through. This is called the blushing angel and is considered one of the more difficult mutations to manage. It shows up when a stripeless is crossed with another stripeless.

Marble Angels

About 1969, the marble angel was introduced. This has proven to be one of the strongest and most popular of all angelfish mutations. Each marble has a different pattern of marbling on the body. They range from nearly all white with patches of black to nearly all black with small streaks of white marbling. The ratio of dark to light is easily manipulated by the hobbyist through selective pairings that and makes your strains distinctive and easily recognizable. The fins also carry the white and dark pattern but in vertical streaks of color instead of marbling. There are many different ways to produce marketable marble angels, including crossing a marble with silver, or gold, or stripeless, or zebra, or, of course, marble. A marble gold cross, I believe, is the most attractive.

Gold Angels

The first all gold angel was produced in 1970. It was called the Naja Gold, discovered in a spawn of black lace. These golds were unusual in that they looked like normal silvers when small and required at least nine months to produce their gold overtones. This line eventually died out. Later, the Hong Kong gold angels appeared and disappeared. The genetic variety known as "new gold" is the common gold found in commerce today. It is a stable, well-established, uniformly gold, and very valuable variety.

A nicely-colored gold angel.

Smoky Angels

The smoky angel soon followed in the early 1970s. It is an angel with a silvery anterior half with the posterior half of the body being a mottled brown. However, unlike the half-black angel that has a strong clean line dividing the two colors, the smoky brown color fades and feathers into the silver in an appealing, random way.

Chocolate Angels

This fish has brown patches that cover nearly the entire body but never all of it. Chocolate angels are produced from crossing two smokys, which strengthens and enlarges the brown areas.

Leopard Angel

Another interesting fish is the leopard angel, which is not a mutation but a blend of other mutations: smoky zebra, or smoky zebra gold. The leopard is a strong fish and attractive enough when small. The young are spotted with brown to black on the posterior half and silver to gray on the front half. As the leopard ages, the smoky coloring replaces the spotted pattern.

An adult zebra angel. Note the extra bar compared to a wild-type angel.

Clown Angels

Another blend produces the clown angel. This is a combination of zebra and blushing traits, with black added to intensify the dark markings. The markings are attractive in that each fish is different. The normal stripes of the silver is distorted into swirls, curls, spots, and blotches. They do not breed true.

Zebra Angel

The zebra angel has a highly variable pattern based on the silver, and I do not know when it began showing up in spawns, but it may have appeared for quite a while and was simply mistaken for a silver. This fish looks like a silver angel with one or more additional body stripes. Some photographs show a strong stripe between each normal body stripe, making a very striking fish indeed.

Gold Marble
This is not a gold marble cross, but another mutation that is pheno-typically and genotypically unique. A Koi angelfish is simply a gold marble stripeless fish.

Pearlscale Angels
This scale mutation began showing up in the 1990s. It is most commonly seen with golds and blacks. It is indeterminately dominant.

Gene Interaction
When we see any trait, we know that it appears because of the interaction of these two sets of chromosomes, and more precisely, because of the interaction of at least two genes for that trait, one gene coming from each of the parents. (Sometimes, groups of genes interact, adding their effects. The amount of black on mollies or the black tail/peduncle colors in platies are the results of this additive effect of different genes). All of the traits explained below are the result of two interacting genes.

It is how these two genes interact that ultimately dictates how the young will look. One gene may be dominant, dictating the appearance of the young, or one gene may be recessive and therefore unable to control the other gene and remain hidden from view. Another case would be where the two genes may average each other out (This is called incomplete dominance and the young showing traits that are intermediate between the two genes).

Veilness in angels is a dominant trait that shows incomplete dominance. An individual with one veil allele of its two has a long, veil fin. This mixed genetic condition is called the heterozygous/condition: the heterozygote has one veil and one non-veil allele. If the individual has two veil alleles, it is a

Both of these silver angels have the veilness gene. The specimen on the left is heterozygous for veilness while the specimen on the right is homozygous for veilness. This is expressed phenotypically by the length of the tail and the slightly longer fins.

homozygote, and has a doubly-long, flowing tail that is clearly bigger than the heterozygote. The homozygous-non-veil always has short fins. Both the heterozygote and the homozygote veil show long fins, with the homozygote having longer fins.

In order to visualize how the genes are passed from generation to generation, the Punnett square is used. This is a diagram developed by the geneticist, Dr. Punnett. With it, you can easily follow all the simple crosses, predict the outcomes, and even set up the crosses that yield the results you need.

The Punnett Square

This simple diagram allows us to cross genotypes and to predict the phenotypes of crosses.

The Punnett square below is labeled with 'parent genotype' at the top horizontal edge and the left side vertical edge. The various numbered areas are filled in with symbols showing a particular genetic trait. So areas marked 1 and 2 are reserved for the symbols representing two genes for a trait from one parent, and the areas marked 3 and 6 are reserved for the same trait from the other parent. Squares labeled 4, 5, 7, and 8 will show us the combinations possible. All of these combinations will be seen in some young. Once we see what combinations will occur (these are genotypes), it is easy to deduce what phenotypes we will see. After the first example, the labeling will be dropped.

	1	2
3	4	5
6	7	8

A basic Punnett square.

How to Use Punnett Squares

The same simple Mendelian patterns apply to all fish. Similar Mendelian patterns of inheritance are seen in all living things, with some weird twists thrown in for good measure. Angelfish traits are easy to learn with because all of the simple color and fin inheritance follows Mendelian patterns.

Alleles

Alternate forms of a genetic trait are called alleles. There are two alleles for fin length in angels: veil and non-veil. Every fish has many pairs of chromosomes in its cells, but only one pair of chromosomes carries the genes for fin length. On these two chromosomes there are genes. One gene only on each chromosome carries genetic information that dictates fin length. These two genes determine fin length in each of the young.

Many other recognizable phenotypes are combinations of characters, or a doubling of characters, and are mentioned in the following section on genetics, while other varieties that are not in the normal commercial trade are omitted.

Genes for Wild-Type Parent X Genes for Veil Parent

The example below shows a Punnett square with a doubly-veil parent (in the two chromosomes carried by this parent, both genes are causing veilness) crossed with a wild-type (Wild-type simply means that the trait is the one found in naturally occurring wild populations. It does not mean the fish is wild caught.).

	1 V	2 V
3 V	4	5
6 V	7	8

The capitalized letter "V" in areas 1 and 2 means that the gene for veilness is a dominant gene. The small "v" in areas 3 and 6 stands for a recessive wild type trait.

How can there be two veil traits? Where do these alternate forms come from? The recessive "v" is the condition found in the wild. The "V" is a mutation discovered among a tank of wild-type silver angels in the early 1950's. It is likely that this mutation has occurred in nature too, but perhaps the long fins made it easier prey, and consequently they didn't survive to reproduce in nature.

Cells numbered 4, 5, 7, and 8 are filled in by combining each gene from each parent with each gene from the other parent. Fill in cell 4 with a "V" donated by one parent and a "v" donated by the other. Fill in the other cells the same way. Thus, cell 5 is a combination of area 2 and 3. Cell 7 is the combination of 1 and 6.

	1 V	2 V
3 v	4 Vv	5 Vv
6 v	7 Vv	8 Vv

Here is the square filled in. Since each parent can only donate one gene for any trait to each of its young, which of its two genes gets donated? Both get donated, one gene to 1/2 of eggs (or sperm), and 1/2 to the other eggs (or sperm).

So what did we find out from this cross? All of the young received a dominate "V" gene and a recessive "v" gene. All of the young, having the same genotype must look identical

The marble trait in these angels is obviously the dominant gene over any other gene that these juveniles may have.

with respect to veilness. Also, since the veil trait is dominate over the recessive wild-type, all the young will be veiled.

Each adult in this previous cross is homozygous for a trait, meaning each parent had only one allele to donate: each one was pure for that trait. One parent was homozygous dominant, and one was homozygous recessive for veil.

Regardless of what the trait is, the results from a homozygous dominant and a homozygous recessive cross is ALWAYS 100% heterozygous (mixed) genotype and 100% dominant phenotype. Genetically mixed, but all showing the dominant trait.

What will be the result from a cross between a homozygous marble and a wild-type silver angel? The marble trait is dominant to silver. Work out a Punnett square using "M" for the dominant marble trait and "m" for the recessive silver.

This is another homozygous/homozygous cross with a dominant trait, so you will get 100% mixed genotypes and 100% marbles.

The same goes for crosses of zebra (dominant) and silver, black (dominant) and silver, and silver (dominate in this case) and gold (recessive to everything!).

Let's follow the young from the marble/silver cross by breeding brother to sister. Here we are breeding two heterozygous adults. The results from all such crosses follow the same pattern.

	1 M	2 m
3 M	4 MM	5 Mm
6 m	7 Mm	8 mm

A homozygous/homozygous cross (Silver Marble X Silver Marble) with a dominant trait resulting in 100% mixed genotypes and 100% marbles.

Homozygous/Heterozygous Crosses

- Crosses between individuals having only homozygous dominant genes will produce 100% homozygous offspring showing the dominant trait.

- A homozygous recessive individual crossed with homozygous recessive produces 100% homozygous recessive offspring.

- A homozygous dominant crossed with a homozygous recessive will produce 100% heterozygous young showing the dominant trait.

- A heterozygote crossed with a heterozygote always gives a 3:1 ratio of dominant to recessive young: 25% of the young are homozygous dominants, 50% are heterozygotes that show the dominant trait, and 25% that show the recessive feature.

- A homozygote dominant crossed with a heterozygote yields 100% dominant traits: 50% homozygous dominant young, 50% heterozygous young.

- A homozygous recessive parent crossed with a heterozygote must produce a mix: 50% homozygotes carrying the recessive gene, 50% heterozygotes.

This group of subadult angels belongs to the same brood. If you look closely, you'll see quite a variety of colors and patterns. In this group, silver was more prevalent than any other phenotype.

Consequently, there are efficient ways to make your crosses. If you want the young to be genetically uniform for a particular trait, then use the crosses that give you uniformity. These batches will require no sorting, saving a great deal of time.

If you need to produce a variety of young from one cross, use parents carrying to a mix of alleles.

Dihybrid Crosses

If you wish to follow two different genes instead of one, you can construct a larger Punnett square. Below is the diagram for a heterozygous marble heterozygous veil crossed with a homozygous marble non-veil.

	MV	Mv	mV	mv
Mv	MMVv	MMvv	MmVv	Mmvv
Mv	MMVv	MMvv	MmVv	Mmvv
Mv	MMVv	MMvv	MmVv	Mmvv
Mv	MMVv	MMvv	MmVv	Mmvv

Our MV x Mv phenotypes have MmVv x MMvv genotypes. Thus the MmVv parent will produce MV, Mv, mV, and mv genotypic gametes (eggs or sperm) and the MMvv parent will produce all Mv gametes.

The young will be 100% marble (1/2 heterozygous and 1/2 homozygous marbles) with 50% heterozygous veils and 50% homozygous non-veils. The homozygous marbles are very dark compared to the lighter colored heterozygous marbles. The homozygous non-veils are short finned while the heterozygous veils are all medium long. Homozygous veils produce the longest veils because of the additive effect of the doubled veil genes.

The table on page 55 lists all of the confirmed genes that are utilized in making the various strains of angelfish. Various modifying genes account for differences between similar strains and even individual fish, so not all "chocolates" or "leopards" look exactly alike. In addition, the combination of genes can produce a variety of strains; for example, smokey and zebra

The veil tail lace is a gorgeous variant that is particularly striking when large individuals show a bright red eye—like this one.

Gene	Dominance Relative to Wild (Silver)	Traits
Albino	Recessive	Removes all but orange/red pigments
Dark	Incompletely Dominant	Often called "black." A co-allele with Gold, Gold Marble, and Marble
Gold	Recessive	Often interacts with other genes to modify color. A co-allele with Dark, Gold Marble, and Marble
Gold Marble	Dominant	Acts much like gold in interactions. Produces a very light marbling, part of the koi genotype. A co-allele with Gold, Dark, and Marble
Halfblack	Recessive	Expression can be heavily influenced by environment.
Marble	Incompletely Dominant	A co-allele with Dark, Gold, and Gold Marble.
Pearl	Recessive	A mutation of light reflecting properties, produces pearlscale trait.
Smokey	Dominant	A component of many color strains. Homozygote known as "chocolate."
Streaked	Dominant	A modifier of Dark with variable effects.
Stripeless	Incompletely Dominant	A complex gene that affects most other genes. Homozygote known as "blushing." A co-allele with Zebra.
Veil (tail)	Incompletely Dominant	Lengthens all the fins. Homozygous veil produces very long fins, sometimes called "superveil."
Zebra	Dominant	Produces one or more extra stripes. A co-allele with Stripeless.

produces "leopard," and "koi" angelfish are gold marble homozygous stripeless (blushing). Descriptive marketing names may have no basis in biological reality.

Many angelfish are crosses that mix two or more genes for color. Here is a list of some of these crosses.

- Clowns are produced by crossing a zebra with a stripeless.

- Leopards are produced by crossing homozygous zebra with a heterozygous smokey.

- Zebra Lace is produced by crossing heterozygous zebra with a heterozygous black.

- Black Velvet are produced by crossing homozygous stripeless with a black/gold heterozygote.

Whites are produced by crossing homozygous gold with a homozygous stripeless.
Opposite: Half-black veils are very popular with hobbyists.

4

Reproduction

For the purpose of this book, I have divided the raising of angelfishes into five phases: selecting broodstock, the act of spawning, care of eggs, raising fry to saleable size, and selecting future breeders. These phases are not strictly different, but rather complement each other and overlap to a degree. However, each area does require different techniques, methods, and knowledge.

Selecting Broodstock

There are potential problems when starting with adult angelfish. For example, you probably don't know if you have pairs, nor do you know their ages, their health, past disease history (including exposure to possibly sterilizing drugs), or even their genetics. In general, you should not use adults as your first breeding stock! The only advantage is that you can save some time.

If you are starting with young—and this is the best way—then you must be able to choose promising stock. This is not difficult, but the more careful and informed you are, the better your chances of obtaining high-quality breeders. Most experts

Young angles need space—and lots of it!

agree that you should choose as many youngsters as you can comfortably house, but no fewer than six of each phenotype. In this way you will learn about angelfish as they grow and develop. If you watch your adults develop, you will begin to pick out their faults or strong points as you learn about diseases, nutrition, and behavioral interactions. Because you have to learn the basics, it is far better to learn with young fish growing up than to make mistakes with very expensive and hard-to-find adults.

Importance of Space

One of the most important things to do is to give young angels space. I have tried growing angels stocked from 6 to 20 in a 50-gallon tank, and found that having 10 to 12 individuals is best. If you are conscientious about dividing the group as they grow, you might be able to crowd them more. However, with a lower density, you have to manipulate them and their environment less. And the less you disturb them, the better!

Maintaining Good Water Quality

Water quality is probably the next most important feature of raising good breeders. Use only aged well-aerated water in order to stabilize gases and temperature. Don't underestimate the importance of high oxygen levels, and always keep your ammonia and nitrite levels at zero.

> "Water quality is dependent on the number of fish raised and the kinds of foods used, as well as the frequency and amount of water changes."

It is not necessary to use filters during any phase of angelfish breeding. When filters are used properly they are beneficial, and when used improperly they are deadly. Proper use of filters, in my opinion, means not trusting them to do any essential work. If you are delaying water changes because you have filtration, you are misusing the filter. Filters, like sponge or corner filters, are useful for picking up particulates and perhaps are good for some ammonia reduction, but they cannot dilute and freshen water. They do not remove any particles from the aquarium but instead just concentrate them in one area, where they quickly plug the filter up. Yes, they can be very useful, but far too many hobbyists misuse them and expect them to do things they cannot. You would be better off having a good array of test kits for water quality and performing regular small water changes than spending the time cleaning filters. Feel free to experiment with other methods, and learn what works best for you.

While on the topic of airstones, I would like to repeat a simple fact: airstones plug up! The force of the air and vibrations cause the granules to shake loose and fill the open pores. If you have a good air filter on your air blower or air pump, then the air getting to the stones is clean. If you do not have such a filtering device, the air getting to your stones is laden with dirt particles that cause the stones to plug up even faster. The stones are cheap and the oxygen saturation is important. Therefore, it is wise to replace them on a regular basis.

Conditioning the Broodstock

Foods seem to be less important as long as basic rules of good nutrition are followed: Feed a variety of foods, feed live foods weekly, if not daily, and clean up uneaten foods regularly. While it is true that angels can be raised and bred exclusively on live and frozen brine shrimp, few professionals would recommend this. I like to alternate as many foods as I can culture and afford, preferring to underfeed at each feeding rather than overfeed.

I am particularly fond of using live foods such as white worms, *Daphnia*, fruit flies, and brine shrimp. My breeders do not seem to fill up on freeze-dried foods of any kind. The live *Tubifex* I could obtain was gathered downstream from a trout hatchery that was a source of gill flukes. Information about flukes gleaned from this experience will be related in a later chapter on disease. I could never prove that my occasional fluke infestations came from this source, but I did stop using these worms rather than take the chance. There is no easy, safe, or positive way of eliminating flukes from a source like a trout hatchery. *Tubifex* worms can't be cultured; they are collected wild, as are *Limnodrilus*, the black worm, or black *Tubifex*. They are the dirtiest of available foods and may be a source of other diseases as well. If you are going to use them, make sure they are continuously washed with fresh, cold water. *Never* collect live foods from your local lakes or streams, especially if fish, snails, or birds access them. There are too many dangerous parasites carried in these live foods, with no way to clean them adequately. Besides, there are too many safe, cultivable foods available.

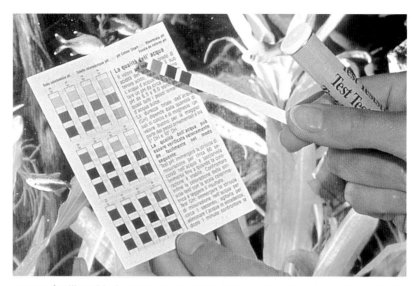

Become familiar with the most popular water tests and learn how to use them. You'll need a good understanding of basic water chemistry if you want to raise healthy, thriving angels.

With this regime of care, the growing angels require little, other than time and a watchful eye. They can be raised at any temperatures ranging from 74° to 82°F. I believe any temperature within this range would produce equally strong breeders. However, it is important to vary the environment as little as possible throughout their lives. In cooler temperatures, angels might require a bit longer maturing, but over the course of a year, it would make little difference. I know of no problems that might be caused by raising angels at day lengths of less than 12 hours a day, but I think they do better with about 14 hours a day. I have no scientific evidence to back this up, but I can offer this information based on my personal experiences over the years, as well as the recommendations of many other authors, all of whom suggest between 12 and 16 hours of light per day. Always leave small night-lights on all night, every night, in your fish room.

Sexing Angels

There are many methods of sexing angels. While it is true that adult angels will pair themselves, sparing you the embarrassment of guessing wrong, occasionally you will want to pair up particular individuals showing particular traits. If you need to do this, it is handy to be able to choose individuals of the opposite sex.

Some of the most common methods of visually sexing angels are looking at the forehead, the ventral fins, the body shape, the degree of horizontalness of the belly, and the distance between the ventral fins and the anal fin. Males are said to have a humped forehead, at least more humped than the females (typical of many other cichlids, too). This trait is pronounced in individuals carrying a stripeless gene. The ventral fins are carried straight down in males and are shifted slightly forward in females. The males look quite slim, and looking head-on, have

Sexing subadult angels is difficult to do by simply looking at them. Males of these smokey angels are prone to develop larger foreheads compared to those carrying genes for striping.

their ventral midline tapered sharply to a knife-edge along the belly. Females, when looking head-on, are fuller. This can be seen more easily after a heavy feeding. The profile from the mouth to the base of the anal fin is straighter in males, but it has a pronounced break along the ventral fins and is more horizontal along the belly in females. The distance between the ventral fins and the anal fin is shorter in males and visibly longer in females. Taken individually, these sex characteristics are inconclusive. Taken as a composite, they are reliable. Of course, the best way to sex them is to examine the mature fish, looking at the vents and the genital papillae. Like other cichlids, the female's papilla is long, stout, and flattened on the end, while the male's papilla is shorter, thinner, and pointed. Both can be seen extending from the anal area, during spawning.

The next best way is to observe them over a long period of time in a group. The males are more aggressive, forming a clear pecking order. The females tend to be more loosely organized and tend to be ignored by the more dominant males. Add slates to the tank and watch for activities around them.

Pairing

Sometime between their 8th and 13th month, angels will begin pairing. There are early clues for which to watch. As long as the group is not disturbed, the angels will evolve a pecking order in which the strongest male will be in obvious control. He will dominate all other developing males, tend to hog the food, and be more aggressive. He will be challenging the other males using headfirst lunges, flaring fins, and other such posturing. The other males may reciprocate, or they may back down by swimming backward with their throats and stomachs exposed to the dominant male. The females will be allowed to feed, will be permitted the freedom of the tank, and may not be challenged by the higher male. They may set up their own pecking order. You will also notice that the males grow larger

Angels usually begin showing signs of pair bonding at an early age.

than the females. After watching the group mature, you should be fairly certain of the sex of all of the members except the smallest and weakest. Sooner or later, with extra water changes and more live foods for inducement, a pair will separate away from the group. Quite suddenly they will begin cleaning an area on a slate or side of the tank, and they will drive all other fish to the other side of the tank. The pair will act a bit frantic, and the rest of the group will be confused and unhappy. At this point you have two choices.

The first choice is to remove the pair from the tank and place them in their own 15-gallon tank. The second choice is to leave the pair in the large tank until after the spawning is complete. Leaving the pair in the tank has a real benefit in that the other fish in the tank will show their genital papillae due to the activity of the first pair. This allows you to check your previous judgments as to sexes of the other individuals in the tank.

If there are approximately equal numbers of each sex, then remove the pair and watch for more pairing activity among the others. If you do not have approximately equal numbers, this is the opportunity to adjust the ratio by adding or removing adults. Note on a card attached to the rack near the tank (or some equally handy method) the sexes of the individuals remaining in the tank. This provides a convenient reminder and scorecard to help keep track of the occupants of the tank.

There is a distinct advantage in allowing the young adults to grow until they are a year old or so, and that is the extra size the females will achieve during this extra time. Once they start breeding, their rate of growth is reduced. From a hormonal point of view, they have shifted from secreting growth hormones to secreting reproductive hormones. From an energy point of view, they are using available energy reserves to develop eggs instead of body tissues. The growth of males is not slowed much by this maturation because spermatogenesis does not tax their energy capacity. However, the long-term success of a pairing is due to the pair remaining compatible, and this compatibility (apparently measured by size and strength) is tested continually during the spawning behavior rituals. Sometimes this behavior is extreme, and one of the breeders may lose an eye or sometimes even be killed.

> "Except for the relatively brief but active pre- and post-spawning behavior, angelfishes act like typical peaceful community tank fish."

The Act of Spawning

Assuming that you have pairs, they should be separated into their own 15-gallon tanks. The tanks should be equipped with a corner or sponge filter to ensure aeration and some particulate filtration, and a piece of slate about 2 to 3 inches wide by 10 to 12 inches long. The slate should not be placed up front where it is more easily viewed. Pairs prefer not to be disturbed (such as by nosy hobbyists) when they are spawning. The normal position for a 15-gallon tank in a hatchery is with one end facing the aisle, maximizing privacy for the pair and the number of tanks for each linear foot of rack, and minimizing the amount of disturbance to each pair. In order to avoid climbing over the tank to reach a piece of slate placed in the isolated back corner (meanwhile driving the adults crazy), I prefer to place the slate against the side of the tank toward the middle and far away from the primary feeding and siphoning area which should be near the front of the tank.

Sometimes, you may want to replace a piece of slate with a spawn on it with a new piece in hope that the pair will either re-spawn or because you wish to raise the fry without the parents help. To do this, slip the new slate vertically in front of the old, then remove the old slate and lean the new one back into the place of the original. With surreptitious execution, the pair will not usually react aggressively and may even continue to fan and protect the non-existent eggs. Their instincts are much stronger than their intelligence!

Spawning Sequence

During the first spawn or two, all sorts of erratic behavior may be observed. This is due to the fact that it takes some time for each individual to develop correct and coordinated behavioral instincts and interactions. Other pairs seem to understand the purpose from the beginning. This makes a description of the average spawning a bit elusive; however, you need to have some idea of what to expect, and so I am including a typical spawning sequence.

A couple of days or more before the spawning, the female's behavior changes. She begins by spending a lot of time swimming near the slate, watching it as if attracted by it but not knowing what to do about it. Then she figures it out. She begins a two-day ritual of slate cleaning. The male takes more interest in the slate and in slate cleaning as the spawning time draws closer. They clean the slate by mouthing it, biting at it, and rubbing it with open mouths. They continue this action long after it is visually spotless. It appears to be a compulsive action that increases in frequency as spawning approaches.

After a thorough cleaning by the parents, the female will begin laying eggs.

Although the fullness of the female may not be obvious prior to slate cleaning, afterward she should be filled with eggs and noticeably rounded. As she begins the slate cleaning, the distension of the body cavity due to eggs will cause the genital papilla to protrude. Look immediately behind the anal opening to find a long, stubby, truncated structure, her ovipositor. Typically, the male's papilla is slower in emerging, perhaps not visible until the day of spawning. It is located in the same relative position, but it is shorter, slim, and pointed. While this cleaning is going on, the pair will show more and more interest in each other. This will be demonstrated in ritualistic and repeated jaw-locking, nipping, mock attacks, threat displays, and probably some loosened scales and torn fins.

As spawning time approaches, the violence between the pair often increases, and you will notice them practically beating each other up to the point of serious injury. All of this is quite normal behavior, albeit hard to watch sometimes, but after all, they are cichlids!

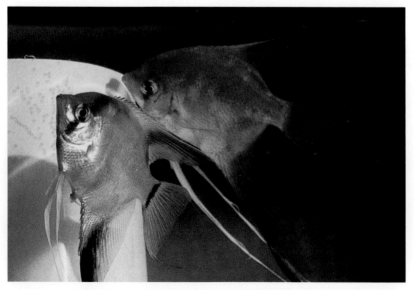

The male will follow the female closely while she is laying the eggs and fertilize them.

Then, on some cryptic signal, the female begins making false passes up the slate. This is done by her approaching the slate headfirst and turning up as if she were going to swim to the surface. As her nose tilts upward, she curls both pelvic fins back against the body and swims along the slate, gently touching it with her ovipositor. Then she goes back to scrubbing the slate for a while and more and more frequent false passes occur.

The same motions made during these false passes will eventually result in eggs being deposited individually on the slate. The male does not usually make false passes, but he begins the same swimming motion along the slate once the female starts laying eggs. She normally places the eggs in the upper one third of the slate, occasionally somewhere else. I had one female that consistently laid eggs at the bottom of the slate, and she swam across the slate rather than up it. But she was the only female out of hundreds that did this. Normally, eggs are laid in fairly straight, long parallel rows up the slate. Sometimes the eggs touch each other, but more often, they are evenly spaced apart.

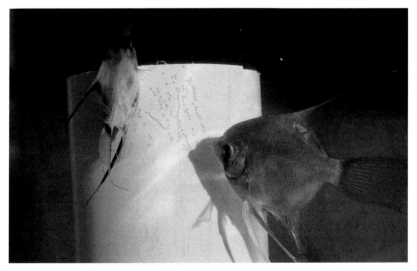

Both parents will continue to spawn until there are approximately 200 to 600 eggs deposited on the base.

The female continues laying her eggs as she swims up the slate until her nose breaks water, whereupon she veers off and positions herself to begin again. The male tends to make fertilization passes in one of two ways: Either he swims with the female, lagging just slightly behind her lead, or he will alternate passes, fertilizing the eggs after she has finished a pass. This egg laying and fertilizing goes on for an hour or two and will result in 200 to 600 eggs.

Occasionally, the pair will take a short break only to resume spawning even more. Just when you think they're done, they start up again!

Post Spawining

After the spawning is complete, the female may drive the male away and guard the eggs alone. She will hover near the eggs, fanning them with her pectoral fins, stopping only to escort the male back to a distant corner or to eat the dead eggs. Hopefully, she will not eat any viable eggs if you keep her well fed and the male does as he's instructed. Often, eggs will get knocked off the slate and fall to the bottom. She will spot them, swim down, gather them in her mouth, swim back to the slate, and spit them back onto the slate. If the eggs don't stick, she will continue picking them up and spitting them back, trying to get them to stick. She is normally a very diligent mother, no matter how small the spawn. She continues fanning and protecting the eggs until they hatch.

You may see a reappearance of the behavior observed prior to spawning any time after spawning is completed. As you approach the tank, you may also see the male spread his fins and rush the glass to challenge your presence near his territory. Usually you should intervene, taking the eggs or newly hatched young away from the pair in order to raise them without fear of their getting eaten. You should intervene so that the pair can resume their normal routine, and after a period of time, spawn again.

It's truly a beautiful site to see a few hundred perfectly fertilized eggs attached to a spawning base.

Inducing Spawning

You are probably familiar with inducing spawning by increasing water changes and improving quality and quantity of foods. However, there is another method that is based on the natural biology of angelfishes.

Both male and female angelfishes use various sexual cues during courtship and spawning. Often, females will lose the urge to spawn when isolated. This and other evidence indicates visual, chemical, and other sensory communication are vital parts of mating. If females can see males, it increases their spawning rates. If you place a ripe female in a tank in which a pair just spawned, she may spawn. Some chemical secreted into the water remains and stimulates the second female. How can you take advantage of these observations?

First, never block the vision between tanks, but instead allow each pair to see its neighbors. Place your 15-gallon breeder tanks on your rack so the end is visible to the aisle and the sides are visible to the adjoining 15-gallon tanks. This saves space but still gives you adequate access, and it exposes the fish to a minimum of disturbance from people and a maximum of interaction and inducement from other pairs. You can also allow a pair to spawn in the same tank (a 50-gallon tank) with other unpaired adults. All of the adults will show papillae and will demonstrate interest in spawning, even after the pair is removed.

Horizontal Vs. Vertical Spawners

It is fairly common knowledge that South American cichlids spawn along the substrate on rocks or other hard horizontal

Angels commonly prefer to spawn in a vertical fashion.

surfaces, or on vertical surfaces, choosing plant leaves, slanted rocks, and outer surfaces of overturned flower pots (in aquariums). Angels are, of course, vertical spawners. However, if angels are sufficiently disturbed, females may decide to spawn horizontally on the bottom or in a corner. A female may decide to kill the male as well, or she may simply jump out of the tank.

"Sufficient disturbance" includes things like trying to switch partners too late in the spawning behavior, or the hobbyist beginning to clean the glass and filter because he didn't notice a female was ready to spawn. These are the kinds of things people do to fish that make you wonder how these fish survive at all!

Cannibalism

With the highly inbred lines that have been selected by humans for characteristics other than maternal care (artificial selection), it is not too surprising that many pairs eat their eggs or young. Even in nature, the young would be fair game to the adults after a period of time. However, if the fish are given a chance, most will properly care for their eggs and young. They need space, though, more space than a 15-gallon aquarium, and they need some degree of privacy without an obtrusive hobbyist getting in the way. Undoubtedly, if young pairs were given the opportunity to raise their spawns, they would revive the necessary instincts. Yes, they would also make mistakes, like eating a few eggs and fry, but nature is so resilient and persistent that I believe in the eventual success of the parental instincts.

In the meantime, do not be discouraged by the failures of any given pair. Your job is to pull the eggs, raise them artificially, and let the pair begin again. Young pairs may still fail to produce fertile eggs for the first two or three spawns, and then they may be good producers after that. If they still do not provide fertile eggs after three tries, then I break them up, putting each in a different community of young adults, in order to pair them again. However, as long as no injury is done to either partner, I do not get rid of them, but instead try again. If damage is done, the offender is culled out and sold to retailers as a single adult. It has been claimed that the dominant male in a community of growing angels is often too aggressive to be a good breeder. While I have never observed this correlation, it may be true. You might keep track of this and see for yourself. If it is true, you may be able to save some poor females from a thrashing.

Re-Pairing Breeders

Re-pairing breeder angels usually isn't a problem. About seven or eight out of every ten recombinations will result in new breeding pairs. However, I have reason to question the stability of the new pair. These pairs often break up within a relatively short time as compared with pairs that selected themselves. Unfortunately, I have never collected or recorded observations to back this point up.

Sometimes it's a good idea to mix and match breeders from different pairs. This will improve your overall genetic variability, too.

There are a couple of things that will help in forcing new pairs. Try to combine them in the late evening, when neither is near breeding time, so they are lulled into acceptance through the night. Also, move the male, if possible, rather than the female. The male is the more territorial of the two, and he is therefore less likely to accept a stranger than she is. But watch them closely! I have seen a female tear the eyes out and then kill every male I put with her. There is no profit in keeping such an animal. I never tolerate injuries because they cause disease, non-productive pairs, frustration, and wasted time and resources. I have seen little correlation between compatibility and size or age of the two individuals. Although other authors recommend that both be about the same size for a strong pairing bond, I have seen too many "odd couples." No one really knows what factors control pair formation or long-term stability, so just watch how your fish act, and react accordingly.

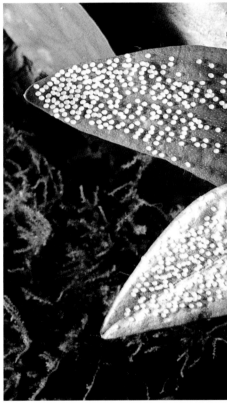

The long, broad leaves of Amazon sword plants make good spawning sites for angels.

Care of the Eggs

I have used plants, such as Amazon swords, for spawning sites, but disliked the disfigurement to the plant that resulted. Consequently, I always recommend the use of slate strips. Large pieces of slate can be quickly and easily cut into strips with a special saw. Cut or select slate pieces narrower than the mouth of the jugs so they will slip into the jugs without a struggle. Cut into approximately

3- by 12-inch strips and then clean and store them for further use. Never use paint removers or any other toxic substance that can soak into the porous slate. Assemble all of the parts: clean glass gallon jugs, slates, and a new airstone and airline to each jug.

Moving the Eggs

I routinely move eggs on slates from the spawning tank to the hatching area without any egg damage. I always move the slate with the eggs facing down in order to eliminate any possible effects from fluorescent lighting, dust, and drying. Ten to 15 seconds is always safe. I have always been careful to not expose the eggs for any longer periods than that.

The water in the hatching jugs should be fresh or slightly aged but never taken directly from the parent's tank. This would only add a flourishing infusoria culture to the jugs, which is the last thing you want. The temperature should not just be close, but exact: Matching the water chemistry is less critical.

Interestingly enough, I have pairs producing very good hatches month after month that suddenly throw nearly all culls. I can never narrow down the causes, but I can't rule out the environment of the developing eggs as one. More often than not, the spawns are soon right back to their previously high quality. Here is where standardization of all methods would eliminate some possibilities.

If you have a spawning on a plant leaf and want to incubate the eggs artificially, it is helpful to anchor the pruned leaf with a bit of lead. The lead should be in the form of commercially available plant anchors that are commonly found at your local aquarium shop. The eggs laid on a plant leaf should be handled the same as if they were on slate.

The white eggs in this batch are either unfertilized or dead from disease. If this happens frequently, consider swapping out one of the parents with another specimen.

Put the slate (or leaf) of eggs in the gallon jar so that the slate (or leaf) leans at the steepest angle possible with the eggs on the upperside. Place the airstone on the bottom, as far away from the eggs as possible. Use moderate aeration. One way to test the amount of aeration is to watch eggs that have fallen off the slate for effects due to currents. The eggs should never be swirling around the jar but should only be gently rocked on the bottom by the force of aeration. The eggs should never be allowed to be touched by bubbles and should never be knocked off the slate by the current until after they have hatched. Once hatched, the current may knock them off without hurting them.

Try the first few spawnings without any antimicrobial agents. If you get good hatches and little or no fungal growth on dead eggs, then you are truly blessed. The rest of us have to struggle a bit more in order to find the right treatment for inhibiting organisms that kill fertile eggs. Let's assume the worst—all or most of your eggs have died. Eggs that die within the first 24 hours were not fertilized. Eggs dying after that period may indicate a water quaility problem. Test your water for pH, hardness, oxygen levels, ammonia, nitrite, and nitrate. If nothing shows up as abnormal, then send a water sample out to your municipal water-quality lab to get more information. If you are on a city water system, you should be able to get a thorough water-quality analysis with a phone call or two to your city government's health department.

While this is going on, watch the dying eggs. If you have a microscope, examine a few dead eggs. Even a hand lens may prove useful in identifying the kinds of organisms responsible for the death of the eggs. Do you see predominantly fungi, protozoans, infusorians, or bacterial clouds? Perhaps you can get the help of a local biology teacher, college professor, or experienced hobbyist. If there is a fisheries school close, that may be the best source of expertise. This is not an easy problem, so don't be discouraged if you do not get the kind of help you need. If this fails or you do not have the time or necessary equipment, then simple set up some experiments to determine appropriate treatments.

Most authors around the country have claimed that egg fungi are the major problem in getting eggs to hatch. It is commonly held that these fungi attack live fish eggs. The belief that fungi are the cause of the problem comes from a simple observation: These fungi are large and easily seen, they spread among eggs so quickly, and dyes used to kill them allow the eggs to hatch better.

"My own observations and experiences indicate that the fungi are never the cause of death of fertile eggs. "

I firmly believe that these fungi grow on the eggs after the eggs have already been injured or killed by other agents. In the typical case, the environment around an egg is thick with infusorians and bacteria. As water around the egg becomes thicker with organisms competing for oxygen, food resources, and excreting pollutants, the water quality will greatly decrease. Remember, the egg itself is a living thing, respiring, exchanging gases, and absorbing water as it develops. The eggs are not adapted to compete in such poor water conditions, and so they die. The fungi are slow colonizers compared with protozoans and bacteria in an aquatic environment, but they are very efficient at growing and reproducing once they have a food source. Because they are the largest of the invaders and the most easily seen, they get the blame for destroying the eggs.

In order to prove this, place some of the fungus-infected eggs with a group of good eggs, and watch them under a magnifying glass. The good eggs may even become entangled in the fungal hyphae, but they will not be killed. The hatched young will attach to the fungal fibers without harm until they become free-swimming. The trick is to change the water often, so often that no smaller organisms become established and create poor water conditions. If the water is clean, the eggs are unaffected by the fungi. If that is so, then why do the dyes that kill fungi also help the eggs hatch? This is because the dyes are often more effective at killing the protozoans.

After all of this, I still advise you to watch for fungi and treat the water when you see them because they are indicators of poor conditions. They do attack dead eggs, causing them to burst, which spreads the nutrients of the eggs throughout the jar, contributing to more growth of bacteria and infusorians.

Disinfection

If you can identify the kind of "germs" polluting your jars, you can make a more intelligent choice of treatments. Some people with eggs being killed by bacteria should use antibiotics as well as disinfectants. If you don't need antibiotics or disinfectants, do not use them. In my case, the best treatment for eggs is a malachite green and formalin mixture.

Ironically, methylene blue, a popular agent marketed for the control of fungi on fish eggs, is a very poor antibiotic, protozoacide, and an even worse fungicide. It is considered worthless as an antimicrobial agent by the medical community because it shows no action against any organisms. Even though fish people still swear by it, I have never found it to be as good as other dyes; plus, it has to be used in such high concentrations that you cannot see how the eggs are developing. However, methylene blue does have one beneficial effect. It has the unusual property of allowing the hemoglobin in blood to absorb oxygen more easily or in higher concentrations than without it, which allows the egg to receive adequate oxygen in the face of deteriorating water quality. This also allows it to be used as a tonic when fish are stressed for any reason.

Other chemicals routinely recommended for egg disinfectants are silver nitrate, copper in various forms, acriflavine, malachite green, and formalin, individually or in combinations. Don't forget that dilution of offending pollutants such as ammonia (which can get as high as 1.5 ppm in a hatching jug) and organisms (bacteria, protozoans, and fungi) can be accomplished with daily (or continuous) water changes. In city water, this might also include small amounts of chlorine that may be beneficial.

Learning to hatch eggs in your area with your water and your fishroom may take awhile. Be patient, and keep records of your various trials. Do not be afraid to experiment; ask other hobbyists and professionals in your area for advice. Once you can hatch eggs successfully, then you must develop a standard routine that includes all phases of spawning, egg care, and hatching. Let me illustrate with my own experience. Occasionally I would have a pair of breeders with a marvelous history of spawning frequency, size of spawns, and egg survival that would suddenly produce a spawn that died. Why? Before developing a routine for handling all phases, I could not rule out any particular cause. After developing a routine that never varies, I can rule out certain errors, or I can relate the problem to a specific change in the normal routine. This gives you a chance to find and solve the problems and can help to remove the guesswork out of hatching fry.

Egg Infertility

With very young breeders or very old ones, the number of eggs may be small. It is also not unusual for the first and perhaps the second spawns to be infertile, due to an infertile or nonparticipating male. For breeders in their prime, the numbers may be larger. Size of the female seems to influence the spawn size, but size is unrelated to spawning frequency. I have seen pairs spawn every four days and other pairs that would only spawn once every six weeks, but pairs in my hatchery averaged about two spawns per month. Pairs producing less were culled or sold, while those pairs that produced more than three spawns per month were used as the basis for legends and tall tales. Angels have been reported to spawn at dusk, at dawn, in the daytime, and at night; every hobbyist seems to have a different story. While it may sound confusing, they are all correct. In my hatchery, morning and afternoons are peak periods of activity for work. Consequently, the breeders are disturbed throughout the day by noise, motion, feeding, cleaning, and shadows. From four o'clock to seven o'clock each evening is slack time, with not one person in the hatchery at all. Then another flurry of activity occurs until lights are about to go out. In my experience, very early morning and from four o'clock to seven o'clock in the evening seems to be the most probable time for spawning to occur. They spawn when the disturbance is the least. Other people run their hatcheries on different schedules, and their angels breed during different times. As long as your angels are given a regular routine, they should adapt to it.

Raising Fry to Saleable Size

The eggs hatch within three to five days, depending on the temperature and phenotype. They may drop from the slate and lie wriggling on the bottom, or they may stay suspended by their cement glands to the slate or each other. During this period of time, organ systems continue to develop. The last system to develop is the digestive system, for it is not needed at this time. By evolving this uneven rate of development for each bodily system, nature makes most efficient use of available limited energy.

By the time the yolk sac is depleted and the extra bulk and weight is used up, the fry have developed enough musculature to swim. Nature has provided the strength and ability to hunt for food as soon as the yolk material is used up and the digestive system is functional. Consequently, the small, non-swimming fry should never be fed anything. They

It's very rewarding to see tanks full of baby angels that you raised up to a saleable size.

can't eat, and food will only contribute to polluting the jar and killing them!

It is very interesting to watch a spawn of fry become free-swimming. Literally all of the spawn will come free within an hour or so. You can check the spawn first thing in the morning and see no free-swimming fry and check again an hour later and find the entire spawn free-swimming and searching for food.

Occasionally, you will find a few stragglers on the bottom. Do not add food to the jar until all of the healthy fry are swimming. This may be hard to judge sometimes. If you see more than a dozen or so young on the bottom, then play it safe and do not add food to the jar. It will not hurt them to go several hours without food if necessary, but all of the fry on the bottom will die if they are fed too early. Check again in an hour or two. Chances are good that all of the fry that are able to swim are already swimming. Those that are not swimming may never do so.

Instinct will help the fry determine what is edible. Naturally, the small fry can only focus their eyes on certain sizes of foods and can only see those particles within their immediate area. They can't swim far enough yet to chase food. The motion of live foods attracts fry and triggers their instinct to feed. This is the reason why live foods are so essential and so much preferred over dry or tube foods. Once the fry eat their first live food, the hardest part of raising them is over. You no longer have a helpless little critter but a young fish that can hunt. That is not to say you don't have plenty to do. The physical work is just starting, and the headwork isn't over either. But once the fry hatch and start eating, you have passed the stages that you do not directly control. All of the rest of the rearing process is directly under your control.

Half the fun of raising baby angels is to see what interesting colors and patterns you end up with.

"However, because everyone has different methods and experiences, you can be sure everyone is partially wrong! "

Ironically, the rest of the growing-out process is equally misunderstood. That is to say, there are a great many details about how fish grow that have not been illuminated by science. For example, whether you are talking about angels or any other fish, no one knows what minimum amount of space is required for maximum growth. Nor do they know what foods in what proportions allow maximum growth, or what minimum water quality parameters are necessary for health and maximum growth, or what temperature provides best growth rate, or how their nutritional needs change as they grow. If you took the time to answer these and a few dozen other related questions, you could revolutionize the fish hatchery business. However, none of these answers are available. Until they are answered, you have to learn by your own successes and failures and the experiences of others.

However, because everyone has different methods and experiences, you can be sure everyone is partially wrong! No one has all of the best answers yet. I tried a simple two-week test to determine how fry density affects growth. It seemed logical that underpopulating a tank would cause stunting and death because the fish could not find the food efficiently enough. It also seemed logical that overpopulation in a tank would do the same thing but from a different cause, namely pollution. But what is under and overpopulation of angelfish fry in a 15-gallon tank? To find out, simply pick a set of logical-sounding numbers and try it out. I divided one of my spawns into three 15-gallon tanks. The first tank held 75, the second held 150, and the third held 225 fry.

Because there was no way to provide exactly the same water quality throughout the two-week period, I decided to ignore these differences and change the same volume in each tank every other day. I fed only live baby brine shrimp and tried to feed in proportion to population. This was done by eye, not by measurement. Which tank of fry grew best? Logic should tell you that on pollution grounds alone, the least dense tank must grow best. The same kind of logic should tell you that the most crowded tank must create the most pollution and therefore must have the worst growth. And that is exactly what happened! What is wrong with this experiment, then? Nearly everything! As you can see, this experiment had too many uncontrolled variables to be trusted completely, such as guessing on feeding, and unequal water quality in the tanks. These problems would be hard to correct. A properly designed experiment should have no more than one variable.

One experiment with flaws cannot be trusted, but the trend in growth rates is believable. It also seemed the growth rate was inversely related to density: Twice the density resulted in half the growth rate. The 225 young were ruined, stunted too severely to recover, and were culled, while the other two groups were saved and eventually sold.

The point is that these unknowns about raising fish are easy to think about but difficult to test accurately.

This little test showed that in this case, stunting was due to overcrowding, but why not starvation from underpopulation? The 75 fish in the least-dense tank grew best. To find the starvation level, I needed to try far fewer fish per tank, say 25. I think then I would have seen some starvation. The lesson is that just because you do not see the effects you expect does not mean your logic is wrong. Perhaps your experimental design was faulty. Perhaps there are other reasons, too. You must think

Angels fed a high level of carotenes sometimes show enhanced red or orange coloration.

a bit about your experiments, as well as the experiments of others, and think about what the results mean.

As far as I can find out, there are only a few proven kinds of environmental conditions that commonly cause problems. They are all either environmental variables, such as oxygen, pH, carbon dioxide, and stable temperatures, or pollutants such as ammonia, nitrites, nitrates, and certain undescribed organic compounds that are growth-inhibiting substances. All are easily controlled with adequate aeration and frequent partial water changes as discussed previously. Ammonia damage deserves more attention and will be discussed later with diseases.

Feeding the Fry

Stick with feedings of baby brine shrimp about four or five times a day. Feeding more often than this is not better, and fewer times than this may not be enough. Feed small amounts each time so the shrimp are pretty well cleaned up between feedings. It is a well-known "fact" that more than four or five feedings per day are not proportionately better. The extra feedings tend not to be finished up. Experiments on commercial game fishes have shown growth rates are reduced if fish are grown with 24-hour light and more feedings. The little extra food ingested is used up for activities that demand high energy, such as swimming. It is only while the fish are inactive that the day's surplus food energy is used for growth (tissue building). In other words, energy demands of growth come second to energy for basic metabolism. Thus, don't try to increase growth by increasing day length beyond 16 hours or so.

Experimentation

I have experimented with trout and salmon foods for feeding fry. The pollution levels rose, the particulate levels rose, but the growth rates did not. I have also tried microworms as a first food for angel fry without success. Here again a quick and easy experiment proved valuable. I placed a few microworms in a petri dish of tank water with a few angel fry and watched what happened under my magnifying glass. The fry eventually tried to eat a few. But this was not the right test to do. The fish here were not given any choice, except to eat or starve. A much better test should allow the fish to choose between microworms and newly hatched brine shrimp. With this in mind, I placed newly hatched shrimp and microworms in a petri dish with a few free-swimming fry and watched them feed. The shrimp were preferred and the microworms were ignored completely! Which food, then, are the young going to fill up on the best? Brine shrimp, of course. Please duplicate these kinds of tests for yourself. Perhaps you will discover something different. Perhaps you will also discover something important.

Many other small foods can be tried. One old standby is egg yolk. Its advantages are its ease of preparation and ease of

Be sure to investigate the nutritional value of the diet you're already feeding your angelfish before adding vitamins to it.

storage, as well as its superior nutrition. Its disadvantages include ease of overpolluting and the fact that it doesn't wiggle. I give a great deal of weight to the notion that fry instinctively fill up better on wiggling food.

Do not mess around with vitamin supplements without some detailed study. They are bad polluters of the water, and overdoses can easily cause disease and deaths. It is not even established that the fish can absorb them from the water. Consequently, adding vitamins to the water just adds more variables to the growth rate problem.

Regardless of filtration, frequent partial water changes on fry tanks are must!

Fry Tank Filtration

Filtering is a very interesting area of aquarium maintenance. Filtration methods are debated among hobbyists with religious fervor and devotion. I use corner or sponge filters in some tanks and no filters in others. The filters are good at keeping down particulates, but I found no other benefits. The same water changes are necessary, and no differences in growth rates are evident. However, I've never set up any experiments to compare them. With or without filters, I get the best growth of fry by providing 50% water changes every other day and keeping them stuffed with brine shrimp. Whenever possible, I try to keep density down to 100 fry per 15-gallon tank.

You may wonder when the growing of angels may require large quarters. There are two ways to judge this. One is a basic cookbook solution. Leave the fry in the 15-gallon tank until the dorsal and anal fins begin to elongate; this takes about three weeks. At this stage of development, some authors refer to them as sprouters because they look like they are sprouting wings. The sprouters are then thinned out or moved to larger quarters. The idea is that they cannot swim well enough to collect food when they are this small. As they develop, they quickly gain the ability and strength to swim farther in the search for food. Now they can fend for themselves in a larger tank.

Another way to judge when the fish should be moved is to note the size of the school they form. The school size for newly free-swimming spawns may take up only a few cubic inches of the tank. However, as the fish grow, the territory covered by the school grows even faster. When the schooling activity begins to utilize the most of 15-gallon tank, then the school needs more space. Because this relies on the natural biology of the fish and the observation of the hobbyist, it is less used, but I believe it is probably more accurate.

A Little Experiment

As an experiment, I once placed 300 angels in a 50-gallon tank. It was their first free-swimming day. I tried to keep the brine shrimp population as high as I would in a 15-gallon tank. In order to get enough shrimp for each fry, there had to be a lot of shrimp in the tank. Nearly all of the shrimp died on the bottom before they were eaten, and the entire spawn died shortly after of starvation or pollution. However, the same number of three-week-old fry could have cleaned up the shrimp easily. They could swim better and could consume more at each feeding.

After moving the fish into larger quarters, begin experimenting with other foods. All kinds should be offered in order to ensure nutritional completeness, as well as to get them to accept new foods. However, their growth rates will slow significantly if you stop feeding live foods, especially newly hatched brine shrimp. I strongly believe that angels should be fed live brine shrimp until they are sold. However, they cannot get the volume of food or enough protein and fats from these small shrimp. After a few seconds in a blender, *Tubifex*, blackworms, or whiteworms are terrific foods, as is blended and well-drained beef heart or liver. If these are not well drained, the excessive blood will pollute the tanks too quickly. Experiment with your own mixes of foods. Whenever you do experiments, write them down. You can't learn or refer back to the data unless you write it down in an organized and purposeful way. Never rely on your memory. It is too selective in its retention and too permeable in its biases.

Sorting Spawns

Some of your pairs will probably produce several different phenotypes. However, all of your customers will want each phenotype sorted and counted upon delivery. Sorting is the

Waiting to cull out poor-quality angels only detracts from the growth and vitality of the healthier, more desirable ones.

process of separating these various phenotypes into saleable kinds and amounts. To a very large degree, you control how much sorting is required. The more breeder tanks there are, the more breeders, and the fewer crosses necessary in order to produce the kinds of angels you want. With proper pairings, you should have little or no sorting to do. But most hobbyists do not immediately have the genetic expertise or the tank space; consequently, they sort.

Because you probably have to sort, at least minimize the kinds of angels you need to sort. Limit crosses so that no more than two phenotypes are produced, thus simplifying sorting. For example, if you need both veils and non-veils, then use one non-veil pair and a second pair crossing a homozygous veil with a non-veil. The first cross will give all non-veils, and the second cross will give all veils. A significantly more time-consuming cross would use two heterozygote veils, which would produce non-veils and veils mixed. This is more time consuming because you must figure out how to separate them back out.

Quick Tips

Consider these hints and tips I have learned the hard way. The larger the young, the easier they are to separate, so a little procrastination won't hurt. Once they have achieved about 1/2 inch-sized bodies, you need to start sorting. If the spawns are large and have to be separated into two 50-gallon tanks, then sort them when you divide the spawn. The way I sort out angels has evolved over a long period of time and works very well for me.

Sorting is a slow, tedious, back-straining, emotionally, and physically tiring enterprise, without the slightest chance of completion. There is always another spawn coming up that has to be sorted. In spite of my pleadings, there will be times and cases where those hobbyists who enjoy abuse will try awkward phenotypic crosses. To be entirely truthful, there are some phenotypes that can only be produced in mixed batches.

Let's assume there are four phenotypes in a 50-gallon tank ready to be sorted: silvers, silver veils, black laces, and black lace veils. The sorting process will require five large fish nets, or you can use floating nets. Place four of them around the perimeter of the tank, with nets in the water and their handles sticking out over the sides or back. Stand or sit in front of the tank so the top of the tank is about elbow height. Use the remaining net to scoop up a dozen or more fish. (Start with fewer and work up with practice.) Hold the net handle where it attaches to the netting in your left hand.

"Given a few seconds to calm down, the phenotype should be easy enough to identify from above."

You must be able to steady this catch-net by trapping the end of the handle between your arm and side while resting the net end of the handle on the front edge of the tank top. Your left hand can control the netting in the water by gathering the netting together, thereby closing the net, or easing the netting back out, making the net bigger. Your right hand is free to scoop the fish out of the confining net and into sorting nets around the perimeter of the tank. Your eyes do the separating. Given a few seconds to calm down, the phenotype should be easy enough to identify from above. Then use your cupped right hand to slowly dip them out. The hand should touch them as little as possible, carrying the water they are in with them. Then move the

Watch For Shock!

Once sorted, you can continue with the culling process or wait and cull another day. Interestingly enough, I have seen people try to use this method, and they kill far too many fish through shock. Shock can be identified by fish that are listless, hanging mouth up at the surface, unresponsive to vibration, motion, or your touch, with labored, slow breathing and rocky equilibrium. You will lose these fish. Never sell out of tanks that have shocked fish; they will not stand the catching, bagging, transporting, and all of the handling at the dealer's. Chances are, there is something else wrong in the tank besides handling: Check water quality!

fish and the handful of water to the appropriate net. Never plunge your hand into the water. This will frighten them even more, and if you shock them, they may not recover. Go slow and be gentle, but be determined in your motions. You know they are too fast to catch, so don't chase them. Instead, just let them swim into your hand.

In this case, let's put all of the veils in the nets on the left side of the tank and put all of the non-veils in nets placed on the right hand side of the tank. At the same time, judge the other phenotypic choice: silver or black lace. Silvers go up front, black lace go in back. Silver veils are placed to the front and to the left, black lace veils behind. Silvers are on the right front, with black lace behind. Work your way through the entire tank, just making these decisions. After a short period of time, you should be able to isolate and remove three or four fish of the same phenotype before moving to one of the sorting nets. Be patient and use your left hand to help manipulate the fish swimming in and out of your hand. When you are done, simply move each net to its own tank.

Selecting babies for resale should be a slow and methodical practice.

Culling

Culling is a far more difficult task. It is a skill that requires you to quickly and accurately judge the quality of each individual fish against industry standards and your own standards. It also requires you to kill the substandard fish. This fact alone makes it the most difficult job in the fishroom. Why is culling so important? Different buyers have different needs; what is saleable to a retailer is not necessarily what the wholesaler wants from you. Most wholesalers want young fish large enough to be eating dry foods, yet small enough to ship large numbers in a small volume of water at the least expense per fish. Smaller fish don't survive as well, and larger fish are less in demand and less profitable.

Retailers may utilize small angels, but the majority of them often want larger angels—those with 1 and ½-inch bodies. There is some limited demand for larger sizes. Consequently, some of your culling may necessitate catering to your customers' needs. Ask them what they want, and they will surely give you suggestions. After all, they want you to succeed in providing the high-quality fish they require.

The method I use for culling has the same net arrangement as sorting: nets suspended in the tanks, with one extra net in which to work. In most cases, you will need only three nets: one net for "keepers," one net for culls, and one net with which to catch. Net up a dozen or two fish and cull them based on the criteria that follow. There are some key points to remember, the most important being size, correct phenotype, body, fins, gills, and eyes.

As you start to cull, you already know what sizes you need based on what you are selling. Invariably, you will want to keep those young that are a little too small or those that are a little too large. These could be combined with others of the same size and sold at another time. You can do it this way if you are short of stock and long on extra-large tanks. However, I think this is false economy. If they are stunted, they will never make strong, saleable fish. Larger ones may have a very limited market. The extra food, tank maintenance, etc., could be used in growing top-quality younger spawns or raising new adults. If you have a small number of odd-sized fish, they take up too much room, and if you have a large number of these odd sizes, you are doing something wrong. Poor breeders, poor nutrition, poor water quality, overcrowding, and poor marketing are possible causes. The best care should result in a very uniform growth rate throughout the spawn. This allows you to deliver a perfectly uniform batch of fish so there can be no question of quality. I recommend throwing out the "too small" and the "too large" fish and doing a better job next time.

The body should have the proper color. Cull out those that deviate from the phenotype. This is usually no problem with proper crosses. Defects in body shape, fins, gills, and eyes are far more common. Body shape includes the overall symmetry and completeness. Often, small half-moon shaped areas are missing between the nose and dorsal or between anal and caudal fins. Sometimes bodies have an elongated look or a misshapen head. Check every fin to see that it is symmetrical and complete. Many times the ventral fins will not be alike. One ventral may be curled, twisted, bent, or missing. Likewise, the dorsal may be bent. Get rid of all of these defects. Check the gill covers on both sides; they can be short, exposing the bright-red gills. If just the thinnest edge of the gills is showing, then you have a water-quality problem. Check your ammonia and nitrite readings. If major portions of the gills are exposed, you may be developing a genetic defect through inbreeding brother to sister. If you are getting more than just a few exposed gills, you should out-cross with another line. Check both eyes for size and shape. Sometimes the pupil can appear very small, with too

What is less desirable to some may be highly desirable to others—especially those wishing to develop new strains.

much of the silvery iris. Usually these fish are blind or near blind and must be destroyed. Blindness can be genetic, nutritional, or can be caused by flukes. Flukes are parasites commonly found on the gills and will be discussed more in the disease chapter.

Breeding Competition

Much of the competition in angels is from foreign fish farms. Their philosophy seems to be to produce large numbers of fish cheaply and not to spend very much time or effort in culling.

This beautiful angel may have been culled by some breeders, but thankfully it wasn't.

The wholesaler who buys these fish does not have the time or manpower to cull them either. Consequently, a number of poor fish may show up in discount fish stores. Your best market may be the aquarium shop that wants high-quality angels and is willing to pay slightly more for them. But don't neglect to sell to these cheaper stores where your higher quality is clearly evident. Finally, remember to check size, phenotype, body, fins, gills, and eyes. Each pair will throw an assortment of culls. The hows and whys remain an interesting mystery. No one yet understands the factors that cause these culls, but a certain small percentage seems unavoidable. The more highly inbred the line, the higher the percentage of culls. The most common culls in my experience have been (in order) runts, crooked or missing ventral fins, and gill and/or eye problems. Occasionally you will find very strange defects such as double-dorsal fins or double-anal fins. Cull everything that doesn't meet your standards.

The Cull Test

A good test for yourself is to look at each batch of culled fish carefully, and then ask yourself if you want your reputation to be based on these individuals. If you find that some would not help your reputation, then cull more ruthlessly. Just for the record, I have had spawns with no culls at all and other spawns that were 96% culls. The average is probably close to 25% culls.

Disposing of the Culls

After culling, release the good fish slowly and carefully, counting them as they escape from the net back into the aquarium. Record the count for future use; these are now ready for sale. Dispose of the culls. Perhaps you can find a hobbyist that keeps large cichlids who can feed your culls to his or her larger predatory cichlids. I use the commercially available product known as MS-222 to humanely anesthetize and kill the culls. I also count the types of culls produced by each pair and use results to help select future breeders and to help track down the sources of problems that may cause the culls.

Selecting Future Breeders

This is a very important duty. Each year you want to add new stock, replace older pairs, and try new phenotypes. Don't forget that selling unpaired adults, as well as breeding pairs, can help you and the local stores. Of course, the new youngsters selected for future breeders must be the highest quality you can find. However, your judgment is limited by the small size of the youngsters of saleable size or smaller. More often than not, the best potential breeders are available in your own hatchery. Conformation must be ideal, including color, finnage, and body proportions.

Future breeders should be of the highest quality that is available.

However, don't select by body size only because males tend to be larger at all ages. This will work against you in nearly all phenotypes except blacks. Typically, black females are small and not very fertile. Apparently this infertility comes from the delicate nature of the homozygous black condition and the demands of the reproductive process on females. I have not heard of anyone trying to boost or restore the fertility of females by using hormone injections, but in view of their value, it may be worth some experimentation. Until the source of this defect is understood and corrective measures devised, use black males in crosses that require a black. Size, in this case, may be a valuable aid.

Selection by Phenotype

Body color and pattern can be important criteria for selection. For example, a streaking pattern in tails of marbles is easily manipulated. If you want solidly colored tails or just a small segment of fins rays with color, select for these traits and persist for a couple of generations, breeding brother to sister. You will get increasing numbers of the traits you want in the forthcoming spawns. In any criterion used for selecting future breeders, you must demand the highest quality possible. This is more difficult than it sounds, and I will explain why. In any single spawn, you are seeing a very small portion of the angel generation. A spawn may be only one-twentieth of the total number of young a pair will produce, and due to accidents, diseases, culling, mismanagement, and egg and fry deaths, the hatchery manager may only see one-half of the pair's production. Yet, even when observing this small fraction, you have to pick the few that are truly the best. You have to do this for each pair and each phenotype, and you have to choose from fish before they are large enough to show all characteristics. Clearly, this is an impossible task, and it is illogical to think you can select correctly.

I consistently try to discourage early pairing in order to get bigger, stronger females and to eliminate individuals that are too aggressive. The most stable pairs are those that choose themselves from a community of young adults. Although you can easily select males and females and force them to pair, many of these will not be stable, well-matched, long-lived breeding pairs.

My success at picking pairs was poor using 10-month-old fish but quite good when using 12-month-old fish. Of two dozen individuals, all will pair if you can correctly juggle the numbers of each sex so that every individual has a potential partner. Unfortunately, you can never guess correctly 100% of the time.

Inducing a Pair

In order to induce pairing, follow the advice given previously: Provide better water quality, better nutrition, and enough space. In order to induce spawning of a possible pair, do all of the above, but add one old standby—boost the water temperature a few degrees. Often, some inducement is necessary to get the first spawn but is not required for subsequent spawnings. This can be accomplished by boosting the water temperature 3°F above ambient until spawning starts. If convenient, lower the tank's temperature to approximately 77°F, feed extra heavily for a few days, change the water, and then boost the temperature to 80°F. This usually does the trick. Apparently, the extra inducement is to get the entire spawning hormone cycles started. Once a rhythm is established, it is self-perpetuating to a degree. Also, angels breed more frequently if maintained in 80°F water than at any other temperature.

Opposite: Albino angels can exhibit a lot of blue, especially in their ventral fins.

5

Understanding Diseases of Angelfish

Hobbyists sometimes have a lot of difficulty understanding the disease process and how to deal with it. Part of the problem is the limited science background of average hobbyists, the bewildering array of commercial treatments and medications, and the intimidating variety of disease organisms with strange names and weird life cycles. The whole mess seems easier to ignore than to understand. However, your success is directly related to how good of an amateur fish pathologist you are—or can become.

Interestingly enough, the concepts involved are not difficult and are actually logical from a biological point of view. While there certainly is the need for a good beginning text explaining all of the subtleties, this is not the proper place for it. However, this chapter will explain many of the basic ideas behind disease diagnosis and treatment and should allow you to pursue your own disease investigations, as well as provide you with confidence regarding your own treatments. Your local retailers may not have all of the answers about diseases or advice about medications. They may not be experts in disease diagnosis or medications and may inadvertently sell you the wrong drugs. Chances are high that in a couple of months you will have far more experience with angels and their diseases than many retailers. For expert disease diagnoses, consult professional fish pathologists or books dealing with fish pathology. For drug information, consult a pharmacist or a veterinarian with a working knowledge of fish diagnosis and treatment.

Interacting Factors of Disease in Fishes

All diseases are the result of three interacting factors. The disease state results from the combined effect of a susceptible host, a virulent pathogen, and an environment conducive to disease development. Each of these three is independent of the others: For example, you can have a host without the pathogen or a pathogen without a weakened host. Neither combination results in a disease. All three factors must happen together at the same time or there is no disease outbreak. This basic fact is now recognized by all sciences dealing with diseases, whether the

Highly specialized strains like this albino pearlscale may be more susceptible to disease than other stronger strains.

diseases are involved with agricultural crops, veterinary animals, or humans. Let's now look briefly at each factor in more detail.

Susceptible Hosts

What is a susceptible host? Any organism that can be successfully attacked can be considered a susceptible host. Not all organisms are susceptible to all pathogens, and fish have defenses that render most attacks unsuccessful. These defenses include the slime layer, scales, skin, inflammatory reactions, immune responses, and hormonal responses. These defense mechanisms working together will often keep the susceptible fish healthy. As a sidelight, the slime of fish is called mucus and is produced by mucous glands. Mucus is made up of mostly hydrophilic (water absorbing) glycoproteins (proteins bonded to simple or complex sugars) that allow the fish to slip through water easier. Mucus also bonds to some particulates, some heavy metals, protects the skin from parasites and bacteria, and aids in internal and external water balance.

Virulent Pathogens

A pathogen is any organism capable of causing disease. Virulence is the term used to describe the efficiency of the disease organism. Highly virulent pathogens overcome all of the defense mechanisms of the host quickly, often killing the host. In order for a pathogen to be effective as a disease organism, it must be able to reproduce while still keeping the host alive. A pathogen that is too virulent might kill the host too fast, lose its food source, and die before reproducing. If it can't reproduce, it cannot pass on its super-virulence. Thus virulence, over the long run, is held in equilibrium against the host's susceptibility.

Environment

The third factor is the environment, and it includes everything surrounding and affecting the host except the pathogen. This

Veil tail angels are prone to bacterial fin and tail rot, a condition brought on most commonly by fin nipping from tankmates and poor water quality.

also means that all stress factors come from the environment. Sources of stress that lead to disease development include injuries, poor water quality, poor nutrition, improper temperature, abrupt changes in environment, or weakness induced from other sources, even another disease. Most often, there are several sources of stress working together to weaken the host before a disease organism can successfully attack.

A New Outlook

If all of this gloomy news is true, why don't successful hobbyists continually have disease problems in their tanks? Successful hobbyists realize that there is a balance of sorts between normal pathogens living on or around the host that do not cause diseases until the environment deteriorates and the fish becomes weakened. The successful hobbyist realizes his most important job is to manage that environment.

One of the consequences of this view is that you can never eradicate all disease pathogens from the aquarium, nor should you particularly want to, with the exception of easily controlled obligate parasites, like flukes or fish lice, for example. Obligate parasites don't quite follow the same rules as those organisms that can live away from a host. They do not have free-living populations in the water waiting for a susceptible host to appear. They are either on a host or they are dead. Other non-obligate pathogens are continually being introduced into the water, being moved around on hands, nets, fish, and plants. They are simply opportunists that take advantage of poor environments and weakened hosts. However, even the obligate pathogens do not simply explode into epidemics. They too can be controlled and held to small numbers that cannot cause damage to the host if the host is strong and the environment healthful. Hopefully, it is now a little clearer to you how fishes become diseased. At the same time, you can see how potential pathogens can quickly take advantage of wounds, skin irritations, and neglected tank conditions. Primary and secondary invaders will use each and every entry point on the fish's body to attack your fish.

Disease Penetration

Once penetration is accomplished by a pathogen, the fish may become diseased. If the fish is strong enough, the pathogen may also be eliminated by means of one of the other defense mechanisms mentioned earlier. The fish could also achieve some sort of equilibrium with the pathogen and coexist without any disease expression. In the latter two cases, the hobbyist never realizes any interaction has taken place! There are two indications of disease. First there is the sign of the disease-causing organism itself, a white ick spot, for example. The second, is symptom, a host reaction to its invader, an example of which might be the fish shimmying.

Viruses

Viruses do cause disease. Some will argue that they are not living and therefore are not disease organisms. Rather than confuse the issue with the pros and cons, let's skip over this to the real problem, the disease that results from them.

A virus causes papillomas on angels. The papilloma may be the host's reaction to the virus, or it may be induced growth initiated by the virus. In either case, hyperplasia, a rapid multiplication in the number of cells, is the result. Although this doesn't seem to hurt the fish directly in the sense of the fish being in pain, it can eventually kill it. The most common area attacked is the lips of adults and sub-adults, and it can be passed from one individual to another through direct contact. I have heard that all of the gold individuals in a mixed tank of adults developed papillomas at the same time, indicating susceptibility in this particular strain. The infection results in a great mass of tissue that disfigures the mouth until the fish can no longer feed itself adequately and dies of starvation. Some limited research suggests this is not viral but genetic, but this cannot be taken seriously until more information is available. In either case, the fish should certainly not be used for breeding and should be destroyed, or better yet, sent to a university pathologist or virologist for future study. Among the hundreds of adults I've raised, I have encountered this less than a dozen times.

Bacteria

We have all probably encountered bacterial infections on our fish. Fin and tail-rot and mouth fungus are the two most common external infections caused by bacteria. Dropsy and hemorrhagic septicemia are the two most common internal bacterial diseases. Until quite recently, these internal infections were not curable because antibiotics are, as a rule, not absorbed into the fish. The most important thing to remember when dealing with bacterial infections is that the antibiotic must be matched to the infection location. For external bacterial problems, drug administration in the water may work well. However, when the infection is known to be internal, complications may frustrate treatment. Most drugs cannot be absorbed through the gills of fishes, and the skin is designed to keep things out. Consequently, most antibiotics never get to the site of infection where they can work. Some companies have developed medicated foods so that the drug gets into the fish when the food is eaten. However, dosing properly is impossible if the sick fish is not eating or is not eating enough to receive a therapeutic dose of the ingested drug.

Common Antibiotics

Some common drugs that can be absorbed into fish tissues, making them useful against internal as well as external bacterial infections, are minocycline, furanace, and nalidixic acid. They are effective against many kinds of bacteria, including species of Aeromonas and Pseudomonas, which to cause dropsy and hemorrhagic septicemia.

The most commonly used products in my area against external bacteria are based on triple sulfas. These are cheap and effective drugs for use on mouth fungus, caused by *Flexibacter columnaris*, or fin and tail rot, which is caused by *Aeromonas* or *Pseudomonas* species. The term "mouth fungus" is used only because it is too deeply entrenched in the hobby to avoid. But do not be confused; it is not a fungus but a true bacteria.

The spectrum of the drug and the gram-stain reaction of the bacteria causing the disease are areas that receive much advertising. But I have found them to be of less importance than absorbability. It is important to get the drug to the site of infection before it can work. The problem of understanding the spectrum is simplified for us by the lucky quirk that almost all common freshwater bacterial diseases, whether

Marbled angels are genetically strong and show a high degree of resistance to common pathogens.

internal or external, are caused by bacteria with a gram-negative stain reaction. Let's look at the how's and why's of the gram's stain a little closer.

All bacteria are prokaryotic, a word that describes their primitive cell structure. All other kinds of disease organisms (except viruses) have an advanced kind of cellular structure called eukaryotic. The gram-stain reaction is used to indicate the two main kinds of cell wall structure in bacteria. Some bacteria react and hold the stains used on them; they are gram-positive. The bacterial cell walls that do not react and hold the stains have a slightly different structure and are called gram-negative. Different drugs have differing abilities to permeate and react with these two cell wall types. A few drugs can attack either type of cell. This ability of drugs to attack cells is called their spectrum. Narrow-spectrum drugs are quite specific, attacking only one type. Broad-spectrum drugs can attack some of each type.

Bacterial Resistance

Another topic to consider when treating bacteria is resistance. Bacterial resistance means that bacteria that were susceptible to the effects of an antibiotic (antibacterial drug) are no longer affected. Bacteria can develop resistance in different ways: by escaping the effect of the drug by finding alternate sources or pathways that evade the drug, or by incorporating point mutations that overcome the drug. Every time you use an antibiotic in your aquarium, you are selecting for strains of bacteria that can survive the drug. If you are using an antibiotic to treat a non-bacterial disease, you are also exposing all bacteria to the drug and allowing them to develop tolerance to this drug. Thus, when you have to use the same drug against some particular bacteria, the drug may be ineffective. The lesson here is to NEVER use an antibiotic against any organism except bacteria, and do not casually use antibiotics in the tanks, especially prophylactically. Change the antibiotics occasionally so that the bacteria causing the problem do not encounter the same drug time after time. Remember, bacteria are constantly trying to evolve past your drug of choice, and the more often the bacteria fight the drug, the faster they will defeat its effects.

Internal Protozoans

Hexamita (=*Octomitus*) is very commonplace but serious in angels under stress from other diseases, old age, shipping, or poor water conditions. This protozoan is part of the normal gut

This discus (Symphysodon sp.) showed a high level of the Hexamita protozoa when examined after its death. The best way to identify Hexamita is visually through a medium-power microscope of 100X or greater.

fauna but can become an explosive infection when environment and nutrition is poor. The fish stops eating, acts listless, hides in corners away from activity and light, and has yellowish to whitish feces. I have set up several experimental tanks in which different treatments were used against *Hexamita*. Nothing worked as well as Epsom salts to flush the protozoan from the gut, large daily water changes to stimulate the fish, and live foods to build strength. As long as the fish eats, its chances of survival are good. After the fish has stopped eating for two or three days, the recovery rate is poor. Only one other drug is useful, metronidazole. Other drugs may work but at the expense of the next spawn or two, as these medications often contain arsenic and will temporarily sterilize the adults. Why use poisons on your fish? I would certainly never recommend it.

If you have access to a microscope with 100x magnification, you can judge the severity of infection by counting the number of *Hexamita* organisms present in the field of view. The best sampling site is any portion of the intestine that appears mucus filled, or any yellowish fluid that can be squeezed from the intestines. A small dab of this material mixed with water on a slide and then covered with a small cover slip should provide good hunting. Watch for small but very fast oval to pear-shaped clear protozoans with six anterior flagellae. Nothing else can be confused with them. More than 15 to 30 organisms call for treatment. Some researchers consider five organisms or less per microscopic field to be normal and not requiring treatment.

External Protozoans

Angels are quite resistant to attack by external protozoans like ick, *Ichthyophthirius* spp., and velvet, *Oodinium pillularis*. While I have seen ick once or twice on angels, I have never seen velvet, *Costia*, or *Chilodonella* on them. This is not to say these

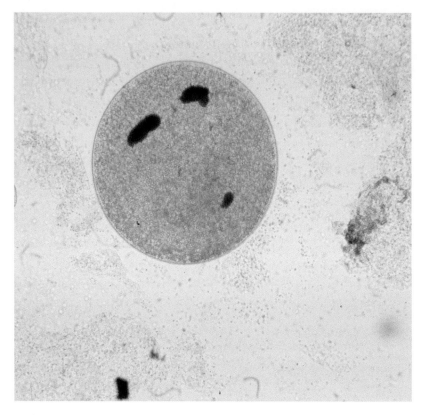

Ichthyophthirius protozoan magnified 100 times under a high power microscope.

organisms will not attack angels; it just means that angels in a proper environment and with superior nutrition seem to be able to fight off these protozoans successfully. If you do see velvet, which is difficult to identify in the early gill infestation period, use the old reliable dye, acriflavine. For the other external protozoans, use a malachite green/formalin mixture.

For ick, it is also helpful to feed extra live foods. Although high temperatures can kill ick in the free-swimming stage, I do not think this is a very good strategy. The higher temperature is also a strain on an already weakened fish. Resist raising the temperature, and use a standard white spot treatment or malachite green and formalin instead.

Fungi

The fungi have more aquatic representatives than you might have realized, with 1,000 to 2,000 species. Yet, the average hobbyist is only familiar with the name *Saprolegnia*. However, there are 35 different genera comprised of hundreds of different species that are easily confused with the "look" of *Saprolegnia*.

The fungi are unique because they do not manufacture their own food like plants, nor can they ingest food the way animals do. Instead, they secrete enzymes that break the food down so they can then absorb it directly through the cell walls. Typically, they are saprophytes, which simply means that they cannot attack living matter but must live off dead organic matter. They can break down such materials as chitin, lignin, cellulose, and keratin, all of which are indigestible by higher organisms. The fungi decompose wastes and the remains of plants and animals.

A Note About Fungi

When a fungal infection occurs on a fish, the fungus is living on dead pieces of tissues. Once a foothold is gained, the enzymes secreted by the fungus, as well as the damage done by other invading organisms, quickly kill more and more tissue until the fish is dead. However, they are not attacking living tissue, and they do not attack a healthy fish.

There are many effective cures for fungal infections providing the fungus has not penetrated too deeply into the flesh of the fish. The oldest cure is a progressive salt treatment. Increase the salt content of the water over a two-day period, with the salt concentration not to exceed 4 or 5 teaspoons of rock salt per gallon of water. After the fungus disappears, dilute the salty water with fresh water over another two-day period. Malachite green, formalin, and potassium permanganate are also effective treatments. Potassium permanganate has the additional benefit of being instantly neutralized by adding hydrogen peroxide until the "grape juice purple" disappears. All of these, except salt, are also readily removed by charcoal filtration. They can be administered by swabbing the wound and fungus, by dipping, or by treating the tank.

Opportunists

Here is a perfect example of using the biological information available to understand and correctly treat a disease problem. Because of the biology of the fungi, you can assume that the fungus causing the infection is a secondary invader—an opportunist. What caused the fish to be weakened? Is there an injury, or is there perhaps a primary pathogen like fin rot bacteria, or flukes, that is causing the initial damage? Check your water quality. Something else needs to be cured, too. Both the primary and secondary causes must be identified and remedied. Many hobbyists have lost fishes because they treat the fungus and do not realize there is an underlying problem.

Quite often, adults confined to a smallish 15-gallon tank will show a bit of fungus on the tips of their fins. This is not a situation that requires the trauma of a dip. Sometimes the fins will heal on their own, and sometimes adding a dose of malachite green satisfies the need of the hobbyist to do something. As a general rule, never treat before you can accurately identify the kind of organism causing the trouble, and when in doubt, don't treat.

ALLOMYCES

Allomyces is a very interesting fungus. It is the only known aquatic fungus with pigmentation. It is also the only known aquatic fungus having alternation of generations between asexual and sexual forms that do not look the same. The asexual form produces the sexual form by way of spores, while the sexual form produces the asexual form by way of gametes. This is also the only aquatic genus that has three different life cycles depending on the species: asexual, sexual, and alternating.

It is exclusively a saprophyte, feeding on dead, dying, or decaying organic matter, and until my discovery of it in my hatchery, was not known to occur on fish eggs. I now suspect that it is very common but unrecognized.

Allomyces looks different than the Oomycetes on eggs in a couple of ways. *Saprolegnia* and its relatives never show any color, whereas *Allomyces* to the naked eye shows a rusty brown or reddish tint when they are in a mass. Also, saprolegnid fungi have a very rank, tangled growth habit, and

Wild angels often need to be treated for various ailments, flukes being only one of them.

the filaments look large and long. *Allomyces* growth is much smaller, forming a tight, clean sphere around the egg. Using malachite green or salt treatments, *Allomyces* is no more difficult to control than oomycetes.

Flukes (Trematodes)

These small animals are very important parasites of fish and other animals, and the limited information available to hobbyists and professionals doesn't go very far in explaining the unique biology or unusual features of the group. Because they are little known and little appreciated, and because so little has been written about them, I would like to spend considerable time discussing them in detail. Monogenetic trematodes are small (from 0.03 to 20.00 mm in length), unsegmented, flattened worms belonging to the phylum Platyhelminthes. They are closely related to free-living flatworms and tapeworms and are much more distantly related to annelids. All flukes are hermaphroditic, with each worm having both male and female reproductive organs. A few are endoparasitic (internal parasites), but the vast majority is ectoparasitic (external parasites).

Flukes occur in both marine and fresh waters worldwide, indicating their success in their niche as obligate parasites. Obligate parasitism means that the fluke is unable to survive without a host. (Fungi, for example, are not obligatory parasitic because they can use food sources other than those that are living.) Flukes have been found on a great variety of hosts, including isopods, cephalopods, sharks, rays, marine and freshwater bony fishes, amphibians, reptiles, and at least one aquatic mammal.

The trematodes are divided into one of two large groups: those requiring more than one host to complete their life cycles (digenetic trematodes) and those requiring only one host (monogenetic trematodes). Many tropical fishes have monogenetic trematodes, and angelfish hatcheries seem to be universally and often epidemically infested with them. We can safely ignore digenetic trematodes in the average hatchery situation.

The monogenetic trematodes are host specific, meaning that one species often attacks only one type (or closely related species) of host species. Approximately 84% of all species occur on only one host genus, and 66% occur on only one host family.

In addition to this specificity, the individual species may occupy very limited areas on the body of the host. Some flukes are restricted to the fins or body, while others are restricted to only gills. Even these types may be further restricted to either the tips or the bases of the gill filaments. The importance of this is obvious: When examining your fish, you must look in all areas known to harbor flukes.

The ability of different genera to move about also varies. In the case of trematodes with haptors (i.e., multiple suckers and large hooks that deeply penetrate the gill tissue), the adult is anchored and never moves under natural conditions. However, most genera of skin flukes can and do move around on the host, crawling in "inchworm" fashion. They move in response to changing environmental conditions, age, size of the host, etc.

While most life cycles are unknown, a couple of basic patterns are common. The first describes flukes that are exclusively livebearing. They give birth to live young by way of a uterus, and the young are immediately able to parasitize their host. The second life cycle includes the egglayers. Egg laying flukes are further divided by how they deposit the eggs, with one group releasing eggs into the water while another group attaches eggs to the host by way of a thin filament. The eggs that are freely released into the water fall to the bottom and develop there for up to a week. The newly hatched larvae then must swim to find a host within a few hours, or they lose the ability to infect and die. Obviously, the eggs attached to the host have an easier time finding their hosts.

Members of the Gyrodactylidae, a large and important fluke family, are identified by several characteristics, such as a two-lobed anterior that includes small sucking disks. They never have eyespots, and the adults have a single pair of large hooks centered on the posterior sucking disk. The margin of the posterior disk is edged with up to 16 smaller hooks. The species within Gyrodactylidae are distinguished by hook size and structure. These are mainly flukes of the skin and fins of fishes and are very common.

The second very large family of flukes, the Dactylogyridae, is quite different in body details. They have four anterior lobes and four anterior eyespots that are easily seen through a microscope. They have one or two pairs of hooks with one or two connecting bars. Surrounding these hooks are up to 14 smaller accessory hooks arranged around the margin of the posterior sucking disk. While hermaphroditic, they are never self-fertile. Species are distinguished by the structure of the hooks and the chitinous copulatory organ. These flukes are mostly confined to the gills.

Most of the time, fluke populations are low and in balance with the host, causing no undue harm or stress. However, when things get out of balance, severe and deadly outbreaks can occur, although in most cases you do have clues pointing to possible trouble: overcrowded conditions, low oxygen levels, and changes in the condition of the host (age, size, mixing different ages or sizes together, etc). Flukes kill by destroying the protection of the slime and skin, making osmoregulation impossible and further infections likely. Gill flukes cause hemorrhages and ulcerations, increased mucus secretion, swelling, and slow suffocation.

> "The keys to handling flukes are to recognize the problem early, recognize whether you have livebearing or egg laying types, and eliminate all sources of reinfestation."

The proper identification is essential because the symptoms might not be recognized as caused by flukes. Watch for rapid but labored breathing, listlessness, hanging at the surface, or slow dying. A distinctive flared look to the gill covers may also be seen in small angels. However, even these symptoms are too general to be able to prove that flukes are present. The best way to prove the presence of flukes is to sacrifice a young angel that exhibits these suspicious indications, and make a microscopic examination of skin and slime scrapings, cut pieces of fins, and all gill arches on one side.

The reproductive type of fluke is also important to know, for although the different flukes are susceptible to the same drugs, the eggs are very resistant. Thus, the egg laying species will require repeated treatments in order to kill subsequent hatches. Complete eradication may require three or more treatments at weekly intervals. Livebearing flukes are usually eliminated with one or two treatments.

Treating Flukes
Commonly recommended treatments are baths in formalin, starting at 25 parts per million, or potassium permanganate, starting at 2 ppm. If these are ineffective, dosage or length of

exposure can be increased. Potassium permanganate is particularly safe in high doses (4 ppm), because adding hydrogen peroxide to the tank very quickly inactivates it. You will be able to monitor this process, for as the permanganate is detoxified, it also changes color, from grape juice violet to clear. Large water changes can also be used to dilute both these drugs.

Another commonly recommended drug is 0,0-dimethyl 2,2,2 trichloro-1-hydroxyethyl phosphonate, which also is called chlorfos, dipterex, masoten, trichlorfon, trichloracide, or dylox. This chemical should never be used on angels, nor should people handle it. In my own state, Washington, this chemical is not registered for aquarium use, and I am not sure how these medications are sold legally here. However, all of the above products are available. My local poison control center advised me never to use any product containing this drug because of its toxicity to people. This drug kills small angels and does not control flukes at "recommended" concentrations. The lesson is obvious: Check the labels on all of the drugs you buy and use. If you don't understand the labels, ask someone who knows or someone who can find out.

Environmental Diseases

Blue-sac disease affects newly hatched fry. In this disease, the yolk sac fills with fluid and swells. The fry cannot control buoyancy or swimming action, cannot feed, and soon die. The sac has a slight bluish-white cast, and the cause is apparently ammonia toxicity. While I have seen this in 1-gallon jugs, I have not seen it in 15-gallon tanks used as hatchers. Monitoring ammonia and partial water changes are needed. Make sure the temperatures of the jugs and replacement water are identical.

Environmental gill disease is another ammonia-related problem affecting growing young fish and adults. The accumulation of ammonia or other products of bacterial action in the aquarium water, like nitrite or nitrate, are causes of this disease. These are very toxic substances, and the fish show classic symptoms of poisoning: listlessness; lack of appetite; hanging at the surface; exaggerated, slow, and labored breathing; not reacting to stimuli such as light or touch; and dying with mouths open and jaws extended. All other poisons will produce these same kinds of symptoms, so you should verify your diagnosis with your test kit. With ammonia, there are additional symptoms: shortening of the gill covers and distortion of the gills themselves. The gills show clubbing, heavy mucus secretions, fusion of lamellae, and aneurysms. If the fish's gills are not bright red but rather a brownish color, then test the aquarium water for nitrites. If the fish's gills are a bright red, then test the aquarium water for ammonia. The impaired gills cannot get the required oxygen, nor can they expel the accumulated waste products. The gills will regenerate if all of the problems are alleviated. While this is the primary cause of the problem, bacteria, fungi, or protozoans may be quick to invade the damaged gill tissues. Consequently, diligence is essential, but prevention is better.

Hole-in-the-head disease (HITH) is more common in Oscars, discus, and peacock bass but occasionally affects angels.

Hole-In-The-Head Disease

Hole-in-the-head disease has a history of confused etiology. In fact, it's a symptom of either an environmental or a nutritional disease, rather than an organism-induced disease, which is all the more reason to be careful about your diagnosis and treatment. Affected fish exude a whitish, stringy material

Angelfish Plague

There is another disease (or a group of diseases) that must be mentioned here for completeness—the angelfish plague. This disease is most often a truly devastating occurrence should your collection become infected. The chances of survival for those unfortunate to come down with this ailment is currently near zero.

There seems to be a lot of conflicting information regarding what this "plague" actually is. One breeder may only lose a few tanks full of angels while another's collection is completely devastated. Ironically, when multiple cases of the "plague" are examined closer, we find that many of the angels have actually succumbed to rather commonly encountered disease organisms such as ick, velvet, or various bacterial infections.

This unique attribute, to allow common pathogens to destroy the host, leads to its contemporary name—angelfish AIDS.

So is it a virus like AIDS in humans then? As far as we can tell, no, it is not a virus. In fact, several scientists have done research on this "plague" with inconclusive results. So, in the end, what this ailment actually is basically depends on whose work you are reading and/or who you are consulting with. Many breeders and tropical fish wholesalers have experienced complete wipeouts of broodstock and young angels so therefore, they have very negative things to say about this and sometimes even more negative advice to give— such as flush everything down the toilet and start over from scratch. Ouch!

Are such extreme measures really needed? Can this disease be stopped at all? These are questions that are commonly asked but rarely answered with any degree of factual information. The truth is—yes, they can be stopped and best of all, prevented in the first place. Here's how.

If you are a breeder then you will need to become very adept at something we call preventative medicine. That is, your methodologies regarding your care and husbandry need to be consistent while remaining practical. It's really very simple; do not overfeed your fishes, perform sizable water changes at regular intervals, keep filters clean, do not overuse chemical additives (manufacturer's directions only), remove any fish that appear unhealthy at once, use only one net per tank and periodically soak the nets in a disinfectant, and never buy or trade stock without quarantining it first. These simple steps, although not totally complete, should assist you in maintaining a properly balanced environment for your fishes.

around or from the large lateral line pores on the head (sometimes incorrectly called "headworms") or show patches of skin erosion around the head. This disease is actually caused by poor water conditions (insufficient calcium), poor nutrition (vitamin D and/or phosphorus deficiency), or a combination of both. It can be stopped and reversed with frequent water changes and a balanced diet.

The other cause of what some people incorrectly call hole-in-the-head disease is actually hexamitiasis. The protozoan *Hexamita* is part of the normal gut fauna and flora but can become an explosive infection when environment and nutrition are poor, resulting in poor nutritional uptake through the gut and therefore inducing these symptoms. In this case, you have two problems to solve, not just one.

Healthy angels should be active and greet you at feeding time.

Resources

ACADEMIC RESOURCES AND SOCIETIES

American Society of Ichthyologists and Herpetologists
Maureen Donnelly, Secretary
Florida International University
Biological Sciences
11200 SW 8th Street
Miami, FL 33199
Phone: (305) 348-1235
Fax: (305) 348-1986
E-mail: asih@fiu.edu
www.asih.org

AngelFish
Garden Apartment
17 Woodside Terrace
Glasgow
G3 7XH
Tel: 0141 331 1617
Fax 0141 331 1976
info@angelfish.co.uk
www.angelfish.co.uk

Association of Aquarists
David Davis, Membership Secretary
2 Telephone Road
Portsmouth, Hants, England
PO4 0AY
Phone: 01705 798686

Canadian Association of Aquarium Clubs
Miecia Burden, Membership Coordinator
142 Stonehenge Pl.
Kitchener, Ontario, Canada
N2N 2M7
Phone: (517) 745-1452
E-mail: mbburden@look.ca
www.caoac.on.ca

Federation of American Aquarium Societies
Jane Benes, Secretary
923 Wadsworth Street
Syracuse, NY 13208-2419
Phone: (513) 894-7289
E-mail: jbenes01@yahoo.com
www.gcca.net/faas

INTERNET RESOURCES

A World of Fish
www.aworldoffish.com

Angelfish
www.angelfish.co.uk

Angelfish and More
www.angelfishandmore.com

Angelfish Forum
www.angelfish.net

Angelfish Society
www.theangelfishsociety.org

Angles Plus
http://www.angelsplus.com

Aquarium Hobbyist
www.aquariumhobbyist.com

FINS: The Fish Information Service
http://fins.actwin.com

Fish Geeks
www.fishgeeks.com

Fish Index
www.fishindex.com

MyFishTank.Net
www.myfishtank.net

Tropical Resources
www.tropicalresources.net

MAGAZINES

Tropical Fish Hobbyist
1 T.F.H. Plaza
3rd & Union Avenues
Neptune City, NJ 07753
Phone: (732) 988-8400
E-mail: info@tfh.com
www.tfhmagazine.com

Index

Chlorine, 12, 83
Chocolate angel, 43, 54
Chromosomes, 39, 45, 48
Cichlidae, 7
Cichlids, 22, 65, 70, 74, 103
Clown angel, 40, 44, 56
Clown veil angel, 40
Conditioning, 28
Copper, 19, 37, 82
Corner filters, 13, 61, 68, 93
Corydoras, 8
Costia, 119
Crustaceans, 9, 24
Culling, 99-101, 105
Culls, 99-103
Cyclops, 25

D

Dactylogyridae, 126
Daphnia, 9, 25, 30-31, 36-37, 62
Deep angelfish, 7
Digenetic trematodes, 124-125
Digestive enzymes, 22
Dihybrid crosses, 53-56
Disease, 59-60, 79, 92, 105, 109-132
Disinfection, 82
Dr. Punnett, 46
Dylox, 128

E

Earthworms, 25, 32
Egg infertility, 83-84
Enchytraeus albidus, 31
Experimentation, 90-92
External protozoans, 119

F

Fats, 21-22, 26-27, 30-31
Flake foods, 25-27, 30
Flexibacter columnaris, 115
Flukes, 101
Flukes, 113, 124-128
Formalin, 82, 120, 122, 127
Freeze-dried foods, 25, 27, 30, 62
Frozen food, 25, 27, 30
Fruit flies, 25, 30, 62
Fungi, 34, 80-83, 121, 124, 129

G

Gametes, 53
Genes, 45, 48-50
Genetics, 39-57, 59
Genital papillae, 65-66, 70, 74
Genotypes, 39, 47, 49
Ghost angel, 40, 42
Ghost veil angel, 40
Gill flukes, 62
Gold angel, 40, 43, 45, 51
Gold marble angel

Photo Credits

L. Azoulay, 56

Bede, 18

V. Datzkewich, 102

T. Forbes, 86

B. Gately, 50

Gan Aquarium Fish Farm, 17, 42 bottom, 52, 69-73, 110

H. Grier, 112

O. Lucanus, 4, 6, 9, 43, 107

K. Lucas, 132

K. Paysan, 10, 40

M.P. & C. Piednoir, 20, 24, 26-27, 54, 63, 89

H. J. Richter, 60

A. Roth, 38, 41, 46, 57, 64, 116

M. Smith, 66, 76, 131

T.F.H. Photo Archives, 13, 15-16, 23, 29, 34, 42 top, 44, 58, 74, 77, 79, 85, 91-92, 95, 98, 101, 104, 108, 118, 120, 123, 129